Eadweard Muybridge

Titles in the series Critical Lives present the work of leading cultural figures of the modern period. Each book explores the life of the artist, writer, philosopher or architect in question and relates it to their major works.

Eadweard Muybridge

Marta Braun

REAKTION BOOKS

For my father, Frank Braun, and in memory of my mother, Tina

Published by Reaktion Books Ltd
33 Great Sutton Street
London EC1V ODX, UK

www.reaktionbooks.co.uk

First published 2010

Copyright © Marta Braun 2010

Printed and bound in Great Britain
by CPI/Antony Rowe, Chippenham, Wiltshire

British Library Cataloguing in Publication Data
Braun, Marta.
    Eadweard Muybridge. – (Critical lives)
    1. Muybridge, Eadweard, 1830–1904
    2. Photographers – Great Britain – Biography
    2. Photographers – United States – Biography
    I. Title II. Series
    770.9'2-DC22

ISBN 978 1 86189 760 2

Contents

EDW. J. MUYBRIDGE, PHOTOGRAPHIC VIEW ARTIST,

12 MONTGOMERY STREET, SAN FRANCISCO,

EDW. J. MUYBRIDGE,

Photographic View Artist,

Studio, 12 Montgomery St., San Francisco

Turn over.

Salesroom, 111 Montgomery Street.

Introduction

Anglo-American photographer Eadweard Muybridge (1830–1904) is a seminal character in the history of photography. His aesthetic and technical innovations, which straddled the worlds of art and science in the late nineteenth century, were key to the revolution of perception wrought by the medium. His crowning achievement, *Animal Locomotion* – 781 photographs containing almost 20,000 individual images – has never been out of print since it was first published in 1887. A figure to be reckoned with in his own time, he would have a lasting influence on art and artists throughout the twentieth century, as well as on popular culture, from the *Matrix* films to U2's music video for their song 'Lemon'.

Also known as Edward Muggeridge, Muggridge, Muygridge and for some time by the pseudonym Helios, Muybridge led a life of adventure that took him from the small English town of Kingston upon Thames, where he was born, to Gold Rush-era San Francisco, where he first made his name, and back again, with multiple stops in between: New York, Yosemite, Alaska, Central America, Philadelphia, London and Paris. In addition to being a leading photographer of his day, he was a showman, entertainer, lecturer, animator, entrepreneur, inventor, venture capitalist and murderer, acquitted of a crime of passion by a jury of his peers.

Muybridge constantly reinvented himself: he was given to conceal his traces, both personal and professional, which has made the work of biographers difficult. Early accounts of his life record mainly his technical achievements or emphasize his role as a pioneer of cinema – a fiercely contested topic in the 1920s as numerous countries competed in laying claim to the invention. Two biographies based on substantial archival research and published in the 1970s, Robert Haas's *Muybridge: Man in Motion* and Gordon Hendricks's *Eadweard Muybridge: The Father of the Motion Picture*, provide fuller accounts. They remain the sources upon which subsequent biographies, including this one, rely.

Haas's and Hendricks's scholarship coincided with two important developments that prompted renewed interest in Muybridge and his work. The first was the rise of conceptual and minimalist art practices in the 1960s and '70s. Muybridge's *Animal Locomotion* inspired a generation of modernist artists, composers and filmmakers engaged with ideas of regularity and repetition, from Andy Warhol and Sol LeWitt to Philip Glass and Hollis Frampton. The photographs also inspired painters such as Francis Bacon and, more recently, Cy Twombly, but more for their emotional resonance than for their structure.

It was also in the 1970s that the history of photography as an art was introduced into university curricula and the commercial market for photographs exploded. Muybridge's place in the story of stop-action photography – seen as a prelude to motion pictures, together with the work of French physiologist Étienne-Jules Marey and other experimenters – was cemented by the collecting practices of individuals and institutions in the grip of modernism. The rest of Muybridge's work, however, especially his landscape photography, was less highly regarded because it was so manifestly guided by the artistic formulas of the nineteenth-century picturesque. The retouching, combination printing (combining two or more negatives to make a print) and other techniques he employed for dramatic effect 'tainted' the purity of the medium. Photographs by his rival Carleton E. Watkins or by Timothy O'Sullivan fitted more readily into the aesthetic discourse of photographic modernism.

The waning of modernism in the later twentieth century brought with it a broader understanding of motion pictures and photography, integrating both into the larger history of spectacle and showing how Muybridge's multifaceted career, with his taste for show business, put him in the vanguard of a new form of entertainment. Rebecca Solnit's 2003 *River of Shadows* and Brian Clegg's 2007 *The Man Who Stopped Time* placed both Muybridge's private life and his work in a wider cultural arena. The first major museum retrospective, *Helios: Eadweard Muybridge in a Time of Change* (Corcoran Gallery of Art, Washington, DC, 2010), continued this change, connecting him to the social and cultural transformations of the late nineteenth century. Meanwhile Stephen Herbert's website, *The Compleat Eadweard Muybridge*, continues to amass and compile every retrievable fact about the photographer. The postmodernist cult of celebrity also served to bring greater attention to the melodrama of Muybridge's personal history; it has since been the subject of a full-length poem, at least two plays and a novel.

More recently, the domination of photographic equipment and materials in the production of contemporary art, the staged fictions of photographers such as Jeff Wall, Gregory Crewdson and others, and the saturation of everyday life with digital imagery have emphasized the malleability of photography, and made clear the degree to which a photographic image is an analogy, rather than a replica, of the visible – an imaginative construction of reality, not reality itself. This latest cultural change allows us to see Muybridge's achievement as he envisaged it and as it was regarded during his lifetime.

When Muybridge began working with a camera in the 1860s, photography was neither the fixed category nor the pragmatic tool it would become by the end of the century. Photographs were first and foremost images that, being machine-made, were believed to reproduce exactly what the eye could see, and with greater accuracy and detail than any artist could ever provide. At the same time, they were also accepted as pictures, images that operated within the conventions of art – an attitude that seemed to contradict the belief in the camera's unmediated translation of everything that appeared before its lens. For nineteenth-century audiences, the visual pleasure provided by photography included both its representational and its emotional content, and it didn't matter how they were enhanced or manipulated.

Like any great artist, Muybridge never separated technique and aesthetics. He used any means at his disposal to attain the pictures he wanted. Working with the wet plate, a difficult and laborious photographic process, he became an expert in overcoming its deficiencies in order to realize sublime images of the immense virgin forests and rugged canyons and mountains of the newly settled American West. He also used his technical skills to become a virtuoso of the photographic genres of his time – stereo photography, the hugely difficult mammoth-plate picture, the panorama – and he was equally a master of the medium's tropes: the landscape, ethnographic description and documentation, and even the spirit photograph.

Muybridge's instantaneous photographs of movement have taken their place with other late nineteenth-century technological innovations that have permanently transformed our notions of time and space. The phonograph, invented in 1877 by Thomas Edison, recorded the voice and made its sound permanent, bringing the past moment of speech or song into the present and forever conflating the two. The telephone, invented in 1876, did the same thing with space, making it possible to communicate across distance and to hear accounts of faraway events as they happened. Now, first with the stop-action photographs of horses he made in 1878 for Leland Stanford and then, in 1887, with the completion of *Animal Locomotion* for the University of Pennsylvania, Muybridge created a new content for the present – a series of instants each filled by a fraction of movement which the unaided eye could never see.

Twenty-first-century ways of looking at photography, however, have helped us to see that Muybridge brought more than technical expertise to his two major studies of animal and human movements. The first image he published of a horse in motion was actually a photograph of a painting that had in turn been made from one of his negatives. The meshing of painting and photography passed almost unnoticed. His 1878 series of cards, *The Horse in Motion*, and his 1881 book *The Attitudes of Animals in Motion*, both contained heavily retouched images. In *Animal Locomotion*, Muybridge often cropped, enlarged and reprinted images and assembled into a single series images that were taken at different times. It is important to understand that his intention was never to deceive, nor to falsify his data or misrepresent it. He was making a good picture, pure and simple.

'A work for the Art Connoisseur, the Scientist, the Artist and the Student of Art or of Nature' is Muybridge's description of *Animal Locomotion*, but it could be applied equally to photography itself. The following account takes the fluidity of the medium – its juncture between art, science and technology – as the perfect complement for examining the career of Eadweard Muybridge: technical wizard, show-business pioneer, popular scientist and artist.

1

Kingston to California

Eadweard Muybridge was born Edward James Muggeridge on 9 April 1830 in Kingston upon Thames, Surrey, a few miles upriver from central London. He changed his surname at least three times, first in the 1850s to Muggridge, then to Muygridge and once again, in 1865, to Muybridge. He never wrote about his family, a large, well-off, middle-class clan, and nothing he might have said about them has been recorded. He remained connected to them only through letters, all of them now believed to be lost. But he carried their values and those of Victorian England with him to the end of his life.

Muybridge's father, John Muggeridge (1797–1843), was a grain merchant. His mother, Susannah née Smith (1808–1874), bore her husband four sons at regular three-year intervals: John (1827–1847), Edward James, George (1833–1858) and Thomas (1836–1923). The Smith and Muggeridge families had resided in Kingston for generations, living in the same houses and following the same occupations. Susannah, according to her devoted niece, Maybanke Anderson, née Selfe (1845–1927), was tender and loving, 'tall and fair and straight, rather precise in manner and speech but exceedingly kind and sympathetic'.[1] Susannah's mother, Susannah Norman Smith (1782–1870), was quite a different character. A strong, independent woman, she dominated the family from her house just across the Thames at Hampton Wick. Muybridge's mother was the fourth of eight children (five girls and three boys) born to Susannah Norman Smith before her husband, Edward, died, leaving her pregnant with the ninth, a boy. Fortunately, Edward Smith, a successful merchant, did not leave her destitute. 'His business is now almost unknown in these days of steam', wrote Muybridge's cousin Maybanke, whose memoir, written in 1915, is the only record we have of Muybridge's childhood. 'He owned barges on the Thames and many men as well as horses were needed for the work. When he drove in his gig to London to buy wheat or coal he took under the seat of his gig, a carrier pigeon, and in his pocket a quill or two, and when he had bought a cargo, he wrote on a small piece of paper the number of barges he needed, put the paper in the quill, tied it under the wing of the pigeon and set it free . . . All the varied work connected with this business the young widow took over'; her two eldest sons were 'taken from school and, well-tutored by their mother, began the different education of business'.[2]

Edward, named after his maternal grandfather, inherited the Smith family's aptitude for business as well, but it was at his grandmother's knee that he also learned to become a proper Victorian child. At Susannah's annual Christmas gathering, as Maybanke described it,

> the providing of good things to eat was not only an excuse for a display of good will to all who prospered by her management but also an opportunity for considering all that related to the well being of her own descendants. After a Christmas dinner at which every son and daughter was expected to be present with even the latest grandchild (and there were always a few high chairs) each grandson or daughter was expected to stand before the family autocrat (in family order) to recite, or tell of work done, or answer pointed questions on varied subjects. Before the time came, preparation was made in every family, preparation which included every detail of health, conduct and dress which might attract the careful oversight of the head of the clan.[3]

The Muggeridges lived on the second and third floors of 30 West-by-Thames Street which backed onto the river Thames. John operated a side business selling coal for the barges carrying his grain from offices on the first floor, next to a large side opening through which wagons trundled back and forth from the river to the street. As a child, according to Maybanke, Edward already presented himself as an 'eccentric boy, rather mischievous, always doing something or saying something unusual or inventing a new toy or a fresh trick'.[4] Tragedy struck the family when Edward was thirteen. His father died, leaving his older brother John and their mother to take over the family business and bring up the younger boys. Four years later, John died while at medical school, and at seventeen it was Edward's turn to take charge. He helped his mother carry on the business, but he had no intention of staying on.

Kingston was a market town that depended on barges or horse-drawn coaches to move goods and people to the market-place in the centre of town and up to London. The slow pace of life had remained virtually unchanged for hundreds of years, but in Muybridge's lifetime the railway – the nineteenth century's new means of transportation – would utterly transform Kingston and village life throughout the country. The change began in 1830, the year of Muybridge's birth, when the first railway, the Manchester and Liverpool line, was launched to routinely carry passengers. Although built primarily to compete with the canal barges transporting raw materials and finished goods between Manchester, the centre of the textiles industry, and Liverpool, the most important port in the north of England, by 1831 the line had also carried 445,047 passengers. Its top speed was a breathtaking 35 miles an hour, as fast as a horse at full gallop; but it could maintain that speed for much longer and carry many more people than any horse-drawn carriage. The coming of the railway changed each traveller's experience of both time and space, as distances disappeared under its spinning wheels and the perception of time itself seemed to be accelerated.

'Railway and Steam Machinery' featured prominently in London's Great Exhibition of 1851, the first international World's Fair. There, in Joseph Paxton's Crystal Palace, a huge iron structure with over a million square feet of glass, the fruits of the industrial revolution were on display throughout the summer. This major exhibition was opened by Queen Victoria and Prince Albert. It included more than 13,000 exhibits from all over the world. Among the exhibitors from Kingston were three furniture makers, one who showed 'cocoa-nut fibre, natural and manufactured', another who demonstrated a mysterious 'instrument for ascertaining distance of objects by day or by night',[5] and Muybridge's uncle Henry Selfe, married to Susanna's sister Elizabeth and the father of Maybanke. Henry was in charge of the Kingston fire engine and had invented and patented a fire pump that would throw water to a great height when, according to Maybanke, 'even a little turn was given to the handle which started the water'.

Although Maybanke, in her memoir, describes her visit to the exhibition, she doesn't mention whether her cousin Edward attended. But Henry and his nephew shared a taste for mechanics and invention, so it is likely that Edward, at age twenty-one, would have taken the train with his family up to London to see his uncle's pump, joining the more than six million visitors – the equivalent of a third of the country's population – who visited the Crystal Palace. Edward would have seen the displays of furniture, jewels and exotic materials from every corner of the world as well as all sorts of ingenious devices, including a primitive alarm clock: a bedstead that could be wound up to throw its occupants onto the floor at a preset time. Furthermore, the *Great Exhibition of the Works of Industry of All Nations* included a rich array of paintings and sculptures, both originals and copies of the most famous examples of the period. The naked female body figured prominently in such artworks, often in erotic guise as classical goddesses, such as Venus or Psyche (Hiram Powers's sculpture *The Greek Slave* received special notice by the press). The neoclassicism extended to pictures of peasant women raking hay or gleaning. British landscape painting was well represented by romantic visions of monuments and ruins, mountains and lakes. And there were many narrative canvases depicting seductions, battles, courtroom dramas and sick or orphaned children. The Victorians were the most literate public in history, and they liked to see their stories in pictures as well as in words. These subjects and notions of beauty shaped Muybridge's artistic vision, from his earliest photographs of American landscape to the naked women disporting themselves in *Animal Locomotion*.

The Great Exhibition also featured photography. Still a new medium – it entered the public sphere in 1839 – photography was both an industrial practice and a new artistic mode of representation. At the Crystal Palace, for example, photographs were used to illustrate the reports of the juries, and they were exhibited – along with the cameras and apparatus needed to make them – in the section designated 'Class 10: Philosophical, Musical, Horological and Surgical Instruments'. The juries awarded prizes for artistry to French photographs on paper made from paper negatives, an invention of the Englishman William Henry Fox Talbot, and to American daguerreotypes, a process invented by the Frenchman Louis Jacques Mandé Daguerre. These were the two earliest photographic processes. The paper negative, or calotype as it became known after Talbot increased its sensitivity in 1840, was an infinitely reproducible negative – at least in theory; the daguerreotype was a unique silver-coated copper plate – a mirror with a memory reproducable only by rephotographing. New York photographer Mathew Brady's daguerreotypes were particularly praised by the juries, who awarded him an exhibition prize. *The Illustrated London News* called the American's display 'super-excellent', making up for the 'disrespect with which they have treated all other nations in having applied for so large a space, and yet at last having left their space comparatively unfilled'.[6]

The description suggests the mixture of jealousy and admiration that typified British attitudes toward its former colony, which claimed to be the most enlightened country in the world. It may have seen itself that way, but it was also deeply divided, with a rural South dependent on slave labour and an increasingly industrialized North. Yet, despite this division, which in ten years would boil over into a civil war, American society was fluid enough that a young (white) man could become whatever he chose to be. And Muybridge was determined to be somebody. In Kingston there was no room to break out on his own. Muybridge's home town and the family business offered a predictable, safe future, but according to Maybanke, her cousin was interested less in security than in adventure and fame: 'He wanted to see the world and "to make a name for himself" and at last he came to say "Goodby", he was going to America.' When he went to bid his grandmother farewell, according to Maybanke, Susannah 'with her usual kindliness, put a little pile of sovereigns beside him and said, "you may be glad to have them Ted." He pushed them back to her and said "No, thank you, Grandma, I'm going to make a name for myself. If I fail, you will never hear of me again".'[7]

At the end of the summer or early fall of 1852, Muybridge set sail for America. In New York as Edward Muggridge, agent for the London Printing & Publishing Company, he took up work importing unbound books from England, having them bound in the United States, where it was cheaper to do so, and selling them. He had done some business in London with his father's relations, who were stationers and booksellers on Queen Street between Blackfriars Bridge and St Paul's, but in New York he got the job through the Smith side of the family, working with his cousin, another Edward.

Muybridge showed the Smith knack for business from the start. He was soon not only selling English books to Americans but also exporting American books to London for Johnson, Fry & Company, publishers with offices in New York, Boston and Philadelphia. And he worked hard. From his base in New York, Muybridge travelled by steamboat up and down the coast with his wares, venturing as far south as Charleston and New Orleans.

Muybridge never made friends easily but those he did proved loyal to him, and a few were influential in shaping his career. The first such friendship we know about was in New York with the photographer Silas Wright Selleck, who had been Mathew Brady's camera operator when Brady won the prize for his daguerreotypes in England the previous summer. When Selleck met Muybridge he found him to have a good disposition and 'genial' manners, later describing his friend at that time as 'a good business man, sound and vigorous of health'.[8]

Selleck had also started off in the printing and bookbinding business, but by the time he met Muybridge he was earning his living as a daguerreotypist. He was a member of the 'Daguerreotypists of the cities of New York and Brooklyn', who had banded together to set prices and who held their meetings at Mathew Brady's gallery. Daguerreotype portrait studios sprang up all over the Eastern seaboard in the 1840s. American daguerreotypists were notably more adept than their British counterparts. They made the process predictable, controllable and fast. And the portraits were cheap – for example, Boston's Plumbe daguerreotype gallery, which Walt Whitman visited, would make a portrait for 25 cents – so a good portraitist like Selleck was never short of customers. As at the Crystal Palace exhibition in London, American daguerreotypes won all the awards in July 1853 at America's first World's Fair in New York. But Selleck saw an even greater market in California, where the 1848 gold rush was quickly followed by a population explosion. In September 1852 Selleck arrived at the Sacramento daguerreotype gallery of George Johnson. The announcement of his hiring boasted that Selleck had taken the daguerreotypes that won the prize for Brady at the London Crystal Palace. After two months Selleck moved to San Francisco. Muybridge followed him three years later, setting sail from New York.

The journey was not one to be undertaken lightly. Getting to San Francisco from New York was unimaginably difficult at this time and took months. Ships either had to sail around the tip of South America to reach the San Francisco harbour, or sail south to the narrow Isthmus of Panama, where passengers were obliged to cross the jungle for a week, risking exposure to diseases such as malaria and cholera. The overland route began with a five-days journey to one of the Missouri river towns, followed by an arduous 11 to 15 weeks-long expedition by wagon and on foot across the Great Plains and the mountains and always under the threat of attack by Native Americans. Muybridge opted for the longer ocean route, disembarking in San Francisco in the fall of 1855.

Back in January 1848 James Marshall, an employee of John Sutter's lumber mill, had found his first shining nuggets in the American River at Coloma, east of Sacramento. In February 1848 California was ceded to the United States by the treaty that ended the Mexican–American War. In March, news of the discovery of the gold began to spread. It was reported in the *California Star*, the newspaper owned by Mormon leader Samuel Brannan, who would go on to become a millionaire selling goods to miners and buying up San Francisco real estate. What followed was unlike any other event in American history. By 1849 approximately 90,000 men and women had arrived in the gold fields in the Sierra Nevada and at the northern tip of the Sacramento River. These '49ers' – made famous in the song 'Oh My Darling, Clementine' – were Americans from nearby territories such as Oregon and transplants from the Eastern states as well as Europeans, Latin Americans and Chinese, all lured by the promise of wealth beyond their dreams.

Before the Gold Rush, San Francisco had been a tiny village of fewer than 1,000 souls, 240 of whom were the Mormons led by

Brannan from New York. By 1855, when Muybridge arrived, it was a booming town of more than 35,000.[9] The throngs of people needed food, clothing, shelter and tools, and a whole infrastructure to support those needs. As the sailors bringing provisions rushed to join in the search for gold, the crewless ships were turned into warehouses and then later were broken up for landfill. Entrepreneurs who stepped in to build roads, churches and schools made vast fortunes. They formed civic organizations and lobbied the capital in Washington, leading to California's swift admission to statehood in 1850. Army engineers completed the Panama Railway in 1855, greatly improving access to the West Coast. Passengers, cargo and mail could now regularly cross the Isthmus and be picked up by new lines such as the Pacific Mail Steamship Company that sailed from Panama to San Francisco.

But by 1855 the first phase of the Gold Rush was over. Now the real money would be made not by the individual mining his claim, but by mining companies supported by shareholders who financed machinery and employees. The other great source of new wealth was real estate as San Francisco underwent a construction boom. The commercial centre that grew around the harbour supported an opera, 40 bookstores and fifteen photography studios, as well as a multitude of hotels, restaurants, saloons, casinos and brothels. The city gobbled up the waterfront, first with buildings constructed on pilings and then with landfill – the broken-up abandoned ships mixed with sand and gravel taken from the dunes and hills. Throughout the city, tents and shacks were replaced by brick houses. The population of San Francisco was a study in contrasts. It was still very much the Wild West: lawlessness and corruption were so pervasive that twice, in 1851 and 1856, men formed committees of vigilance that competed with elected city officials to dispense law and order. The population was young – the mean age of adult males was 31[10] – and a massive gender imbalance meant that in 1852 men outnumbered women seven to one. In addition, the majority of women in the initial wave of the Gold Rush were single, most of them prostitutes. The ill-paid labour force included many Chinese, who were the object of virulent racial discrimination. At the same time, young men from the East Coast settled in the city, entered politics and introduced a cultural sophistication they had learned in the theatres, opera houses and art galleries frequented back home.

It was in this vortex of urban growth and cultural expansion that Muybridge opened a bookstore in 1855 at 113 Montgomery Street in the centre of the city. The building also housed a moneylender/ real estate agent and a dentist. Muybridge quickly became part of San Francisco's commercial life. He specialized in sales by subscription for editions such as Appleton's *New American Cyclopedia* and a new *History of the United States* that came out in monthly fascicles. By the end of April 1856 Muybridge had placed three ads in the San Francisco *Bulletin* for a 'gentleman to canvas for subscribers for a new illustrated standard work'. The ads were signed E. J. Muggridge. But by 19 May the name at the bottom of the ad had become E. J. Muygridge. Claiming 'a larger assortment of handsomely gotten up Illustrated Works than any other house in California . . . bound in various styles of elegant and superb bindings', E. J. Muygridge also appealed to 'gentlemen furnishing Libraries', elaborating on the range of subjects that could be purchased through him by 'our agents in London, Paris and New York'.

He also acquired and sold images. In August 1856 he placed a notice in San Francisco's *Daily Evening Bulletin* offering a portrait 'drawn on stone' from a 'Daguerreotype in possession of the family' of the paper's founder, James King 'of William' – a regal-sounding title intended to distinguish the publisher from other men with the same name (William was his father's name). One of the city's most prominent figures, and its most outspoken opponent of political corruption, King had attacked city supervisor James Casey in an editorial in the *Bulletin* the previous May, accusing

Casey of stuffing ballot boxes and revealing that he had spent time in Sing Sing. A few days later Casey shot King in cold blood, making an instant martyr of his opponent. Casey was seized by the vigilantes and hanged within the week. By placing his ad in the *Bulletin* Muybridge managed to align himself not only with the forces of vigilante justice, but with one of the most prominent daguerreotypists in San Francisco, Robert Vance. Vance had made the original King daguerreotype, which was owned by the family, who permitted additional images to be engraved from it in the aftermath of the murder.

Vance, whose studio happened to be near Muybridge's office, was one of the first photographers to depict the Western landscape, its miners, towns and settlers. By chance, he also hired the young photographer whom Muybridge would later consider his greatest rival, Carleton E. Watkins.

Muybridge's inventory of individual engravings and 'the finest collection of English and American Illustrated Standard Works . . . ever opened on the Pacific' included John James Audubon's *Birds of America*; illustrated volumes of Shakespeare; engravings of Hogarth's works; Vernon's *Gallery of British Art*, the group of pictures that would form the collection of the Tate Gallery; *Finden's Beauties of Moore*, engravings of the heroines of the Irish poet and balladeer Thomas Moore; *Lodge's Portraits*, 240 engravings of illustrious Britons; and *Flowers of Loveliness*, engravings illustrating the poems of the Countess of Blessington, almost all of which depict two women together, a subject that Muybridge himself would later turn to in his famous *Animal Locomotion* photographs. Then there were books with illustrations of the Crystal Palace and the landscapes of Switzerland, Canada and France along with Bartlett's *Palestine* and Payne's *Pictorial World*. But lavishly engraved books were only part of his stock. Muybridge also sold Baxter's Oil Prints, popular hand-coloured engravings tinted by a process that had been licensed to one Mr Le Blond in Muybridge's home town

of Kingston, along with sheet music, lithographs, chromolitho-
graphs and photographs.

The images Muybridge sold were typically Victorian in both
style and subject matter. The majestic Alps, the ruins of English
abbeys, the lakes of Switzerland and the old cities of France had,
since the coming of the railway in Europe, become the purview
of the middle-class traveller, and wealthy Americans who made
the pilgrimage to Europe were captivated as much by the scenic
beauties of the landscape as by the sense of the past that these
cities and ruins evoked. The demand for such images was strong.
Buyers wanted an idealized European countryside, an artfully
designed nature that could be read like a picture, with clear
compositional elements – nothing too wild or surprising, and a
balancing of light and shade that would contribute to the overall
pictorial harmony. Pictures with atmospheric effects, such as fog
or moonlight, sold especially well.

Muybridge's business expanded throughout the late 1850s.
He exhibited his books at the first Mechanics Fair held in San
Francisco in September 1857 (where Silas Selleck had entered his
photographs in the competition for medals and diplomas) and
at the second in 1858, where he also sold steel-plate engravings.
His status as a member of the city's business community rose.
In January 1858 he was elected to the board of directors of the
San Francisco Mercantile Library Association. The association,
considered 'one of the best, and certainly the most admirably
conducted institution in the city', sponsored debates, readings
and lectures and oversaw a lending library.[11] It had the largest
membership in the city, except perhaps that of the fire department,
and the election was highly contested;[12] more than 700 votes were
cast for the nine seats on the board.

Muybridge continued to place ads for a salesman throughout
1857. In April 1858 he moved into new offices at 163 Clay Street,
in the same building that housed Selleck's expanded and lavish

photography gallery. Selleck sold photographs, ambrotypes and daguerreotypes, and Muybridge seems to have increased his own photography inventory at this time. One advertisement in the *Daily Alta California* in December 1858 describes a photograph by Watkins that Muybridge was offering:

> We are indebted to Mr Watkins, photographic artist, of 166 Clay street, for a very beautiful photograph of the Golden Gate, taken from Telegraph Hill. The picture is the first and only one that has ever come under our notice that gives a perfect delineation of the beautiful passage-way that connects San Francisco harbor with the ocean, together with the surrounding landscape on either side. It takes in the houses on the north-western slope of Telegraph Hill, North Beach, and those on the north-eastern slope of Russian Hill. In fact, the picture is a most perfect one in every respect, and will be valued by all who desire to procure views in California for preservation. It is for sale by Mr E. J. Muygridge, at his store, on Clay street, a few doors above Montgomery.[13]

Muybridge's brother George arrived from England that year, but George died soon after of tuberculosis contracted before he had left. When his youngest brother, Thomas, arrived in 1859, Muybridge handed over the business to him. Throughout the year, ads in the *Bulletin* announced a going-out-of-business book and picture sale, and on 15 May 1860 Muybridge placed a large declaration in the newspaper:

> I have this day sold to my brother, Thomas S. Muygridge, my entire stock of Books, Engravings, etc. and respectfully request a continuance of public patronage in his favour. After my return from the Yosemite, I shall on 5TH June, leave for New York, London, Paris, Rome, Berlin, Vienna, etc. and all orders

or commissions for the purchase of Works of Literature or Art entrusted to me, will be properly attended to on the following terms: all amounts under $500, 10 percent; between $500 and $1,000, 5 percent; over $1,000, 2 per cent.

Muybridge's plan was to visit Yosemite, sail to New York and then continue on to England. But he didn't go to Yosemite and he didn't leave San Francisco on 5 June; he continued to solicit subscribers in the 12 and 15 June issues of the *Bulletin*. And he didn't sail to New York. Instead, on 2 July and for reasons unknown, he took the Butterfield Overland Mail coach across the country.

En route, an accident occurred that would have profound and far-reaching effects on Muybridge's life. While descending a steep hill outside Mountain Station, Texas, the brakes failed on the coach carrying Muybridge and six other passengers. In his frantic efforts to stop the careering horses, the driver veered off the road and hit a tree, killing a passenger by the name of Mackey and injuring everyone else. In his own account of the accident, Muybridge described how he attempted to slash the canvas at the back of the coach in order to escape and then lost consciousness when the stagecoach hit the tree. 'I recollected nothing for nine days, when I found myself lying on a bed at Fort Smith [Arkansas], 180 miles from the place. I found a scar on my head. I had double vision – saw two objects at once; had no sense of smell or taste; also had confused ideas.'[14]

These acute symptoms continued for three months. Sometime during that period he managed to reach New York. In the late summer or fall he set sail for London. There, through family connections, he consulted Dr William Gull, Queen Victoria's physician, the discoverer of hypothyroidism and, by some accounts, Jack the Ripper.[15] Gull liked to prescribe fresh air and exercise for his patients, a regimen which Muybridge presumably obeyed. While undergoing treatment he stayed with his mother in Kennington;

she had left Kingston for this south London suburb to live in the house of her youngest brother, at the same time that Muybridge had left for America. Although he could work and travel again by the winter, Muybridge had never completely recovered from the accident; he would continue to suffer headaches and episodes of double vision throughout his life.

Muybridge was well enough in the spring of 1861 to return to New York and pursue his lawsuit against the Butterfield Overland Mail Company. He asked for $10,000 in damages; the court granted him $2,500. With this sum, and seeking distance from the tensions of the American Civil War which had broken out in April, he returned to London – this time lodging with his mother's sister, Rachel, in St John's Wood.

Although Muybridge's movements during these years have proved difficult to trace, he was evidently occupied with many projects, including learning, or perfecting his knowledge of, photography. In the summer of 1862 he exhibited two inventions at the International Exhibition that took place in London. The first, patented on 28 September 1860, was for 'an improved method of and apparatus for plate printing'. Because it was signed by 'E. Muggeridge of New York', and because it was unlikely that he had been working on patent applications so soon after his accident, it was probably something he had applied for before he left for San Francisco. The second patent, applied for on 1 August 1861, was for a washing machine.

The 1862 fair, known as the Great London Exposition, was held in South Kensington, where the Science and Natural History Museums now stand. Staged with profits from the 1851 Crystal Palace exhibition, the fair included 28,000 exhibitors from 36 countries. The originality of Muybridge's plate-printing apparatus was that the ink was introduced from underneath the plate by perforations. His washing machine was based on the principle of a fulling mill. Both inventions, however, seem to have been refinements of products already in use. As he wrote to his uncle Henry on 17 August 1861, 'I am in *fact*, and I think I would be so considered in law, the inventor of *both* machines as laid down and described. And I think were a patent granted me, I could sustain any action for infringement on the principle I might bring against subsequent applicants.'[16] Muybridge shared Henry's inclination for invention, as his many future patents would attest. Neither a gifted mechanic nor an accomplished draughtsman, he was able to get his ideas down on paper well enough to be used as reference by a carpenter or machinist. His ideas usually had practical and lucrative applications. He suggested to Henry, for example, that it would be profitable for him to patent the washing machine in the colonies. Ill health and his inability to pay the costs of an engineering apprenticeship for his son Norman had led Henry to emigrate to Sydney in 1854, part of a mass exodus of middle-class Britons who, reacting to the increasingly dense population of London and the concomitant rise in poverty and crime, fled to Australia. There, Henry's children would become famous, Maybanke as the country's leader of women's suffrage, and her brother Norman as its foremost engineer.

In the same letter to his uncle, Muybridge informed Henry that he would soon be leaving for the Continent 'on business' that might detain him for some months. From that point until 1862 we have only sporadic news of his whereabouts. In a section titled 'Movements of Californians',[17] the *Daily Alta California* notes Muybridge's appearance in Paris in late October of that year, and his subsequent return to London. We hear nothing of him in 1863, and then he is reported to be in Paris again in 1864.

In July 1865 a notice for a stock offering posted in *The Times* of London lists 'Edwd. J. Muybridge (late of California)' as one of the directors of the Austin Consolidated Silver Mines Company Limited. In November another series of notices appeared in Irish and Scottish newspapers for 20,000 shares of stock for sale by the Ottoman Company to capitalize the Bank of Turkey, again with the name 'Edward J. Muybridge, Esq. (late Merchant, San Francisco)' listed as one of the directors.[18] Both ventures collapsed in the banking crisis that hit England that year, and Muybridge chaired the two general meetings of the Bank of Turkey shareholders (24 April and 17 May 1866) which dissolved the company. In July he oversaw the dissolution of the Silver Mines Company. His days as a venture capitalist were short-lived, but the latest variation in his surname would stick.

2

Helios in America

Whether spurred by the crash of his stock ventures or his belief that postbellum San Francisco would be a better place than England in which to establish a new avocation, Muybridge, nearing 40, returned to America in late 1866 or early 1867. When he reappeared it was not only with his new name, but also with a new profession: Edw. J. Muybridge was now a photographer, practising under the *nom d'image* 'Helios'.

A photograph of him taken around this time shows a straggly beard, high forehead and the face of a dreamer with deep-set eyes gazing intensely into space. A remarkable characteristic of Muybridge's personality was his ability to meld his creative vision and his business acumen. Into his role as Helios the photographer, Muybridge would seamlessly fold his erstwhile role as Muygridge the bookseller. He used the same techniques – and with equal success – to promote and sell his photographs, which from the outset were accomplished works.

But when and where did he learn the medium? In 1881, Muybridge recounted that he 'came to California in 1855 and most of the time since and all of the time since 1860 . . . had been diligently, and at the same time studiously, engaged in photography'.[1] Perhaps he began by helping out his friend Selleck. Certainly he took up photography seriously while recuperating from his accident. Dr Gull had prescribed exercise and fresh air, and although Muybridge evidently complied, it is likely that he would have found a way to make such excursions serve a more productive purpose, having been raised in a family that held idleness to be a vice. In her memoir, Maybanke provides the name of a possible early teacher. She recalls Mr Brown, the town beadle, whose job it was to give 'notice of events, past or to come, all with the same implication of great importance'. Brown was 'much too interested in many schemes and inventions to pay attention to the business of "making money"', Maybanke writes, and one of these schemes was photography, 'making experiments in using glass instead of the polished plate on which daguerreotypes were taken'. Maybanke's mother 'became interested in the business', letting Brown photograph Maybanke and her youngest son Harry. Brown's picture of Harry did take a prize at a London exhibition, according to Maybanke, so Brown would seem a good candidate to have been Muybridge's first instructor in the medium.

What is certain is that by the time Muybridge returned to San Francisco he was already an expert in the collodion wet-plate process – photography on glass. Another Englishman, Frederick Scott Archer, had invented the process in 1851. Rather than using paper as the support for the negative image, he used glass that he coated with a mixture of gun cotton and ether, sensitized with a bath of silver nitrate and then exposed in the camera. Although this sounds simple enough, it was actually very cumbersome and difficult. The gun cotton and ether mixture was dangerous if combined badly. It had to be coated evenly on the glass plate, an operation equivalent to spreading a crepe mixture thinly over a frying pan, so as to cover the entire surface without bubbles or lumps. If the coating was applied poorly, the collodion would be streaked and the negatives spoiled. The tilting, rotating and slight shaking of the glass plate required flexible wrists and a lot of practice. But coating was only the first step. The plate also had to be exposed, developed and washed before the collodion dried. These manoeuvres increased the risk of breaking the glass, which, because there were no enlargers at that time, ranged in size from 5 × 7 inches (12.7 × 17.8 cm) to the 'mammoth' plate of 20 × 24 inches (50.8 × 61 cm). Professionals working in a portrait studio outfitted their space with the necessary glass, chemicals and water with little difficulty. But for the photographer who wanted to work out of doors, the camera or cameras, the glass plates, the coating, sensitizing and developing chemicals, the water and, finally, a tent that would serve as a darkroom had to be carried to the site.

Cumbersome as it was, however, the wet plate was a distinct improvement over earlier processes because it combined the best features of each: the glass negative gave the sharp detail that was the hallmark of the daguerreotype and absent from the fuzzy calotype; but like the latter, it could be used to make any number of prints, whereas the biggest drawback of the daguerreotype was its uniqueness. Finally, the wet-plate process was much faster than either of its predecessors.

The advent of the wet-plate negative signalled the first step in the transformation of photography into an industrialized medium. Glass-plate negatives were easily printed, a prerequisite if the photographer wanted to sell multiple copies of his subject. The wet-plate photographic process gave rise to new photographic types. One of the first – called 'ambrotype' – wasn't a print at all, but an alternative to the daguerreotype, still the most popular form of photography in America before the Civil War. Flattened against a jet-black background, or with its back painted black, the wet-plate glass negative appeared as a positive. Ambrotypes imitated daguerreotypes in their compact size, physiognomic detail and presentation in elaborate frames, but they were cheaper and required less exposure time.

The ease with which any number of positive prints could be produced from the wet-plate negative led to another form of portraiture, the carte-de-visite. As the name suggests, these images were roughly the size of small visiting cards, but because they were so cheap to produce they became a more affordable form of mass-market portraiture than even the ambrotype. The glass plate used for the carte-de-visite was placed in a dedicated camera that had between six and eight lenses. With exposure times reduced to a few seconds – taking off the lens caps, counting off the seconds and then recapping the lenses was the usual way of exposing the plate – up to eight images could be made simultaneously on the same plate. This meant that eight images could be printed in the time usually taken to make one, a much more profitable venture.

Cartes-de-visite were contact prints. They were made in the sunlight, the negative sandwiched against the paper in a printing frame, and the slow emergence of the picture watched and controlled by checking intermittently until it was ready. The task of printing, which required patience but no special skills, was frequently assigned to women. Albumen paper – which was basically just a thin writing paper – was used to make the prints. The photographic image was suspended on the surface in the albumen (egg white) coating rather than embedded in the paper fibres. That meant that the image was glossy, not matte, and a final toning gave the picture a sepia colour. Cartes-de-visite were produced in the hundreds of thousands, with the name of the photographer or the studio usually printed on the cardboard backs. Because cartes-de-visite were so desirable, a side industry sprang up – the manufacture of albums in which to display them. In these albums, carte-de-visite portraits of family members were shown side by side with celebrity portraits, which now began appearing for the first time.

In San Francisco Muybridge rejoined Silas Selleck, this time at his new Cosmopolitan Gallery at 415 Montgomery Street. Selleck was advertising daguerreotype and ambrotype portraits as well as cartes-de-visite in the *Bulletin*. Muybridge, however, did not pursue portrait photography, which required a certain empathy with one's subjects to draw them out. He was more at home with inanimate subjects, such as the urban and natural environments. His first photographs were of San Francisco, which had blossomed in the years he had been away. With the promise of a transcontinental railroad binding the city to the rest of the country, there was a high demand for pictures from Easterners who were avid for a glimpse of the burgeoning cityscape. Untouched by the Civil War, San Francisco now had a population of more than 100,000, and the expectation of an influx of wealthy Easterners brought by the railroad. Muybridge easily slipped back into the energetic and optimistic city.

A Helios' Flying Studio cabinet card from 1870.

He travelled in Helios's 'Flying Studio'. This two-wheeled canvas-topped chariot drawn by a single horse was marked on the back with the photographer's logo: a winged camera lit by a bright sun marked with the name of the sun god Helios. The cart held his plates, cameras, chemicals and water and a tent that served as his darkroom. Operating out of his Flying Studio, he photographed San Francisco's prominent buildings: stores, banks, houses and schools – St Mary's College, still a noted landmark on the Oakland side of the Bay, had just opened. He also photographed military forts and prisons as well as the boats in the harbour, the city's gardens and the Bay.

Muybridge published his *San Francisco Views* as stereo cards, another innovation of the wet-plate era that surpassed even the cartes-de-visite in popularity. Stereos were made with a twin-lens camera, the two lenses separated from each other by the approximate distance between the eyes. The two negatives – which were not quite the same – were printed, and then the two prints glued side by side on a single piece of board. Seen in a stereoscopic viewer, the pictures reconstituted binocular vision in its depth. Stereos became a nineteenth-century craze, and stereo viewers were to be found in virtually every middle-class American parlour. There, in the safety of one's home, one could devour images of other, more exotic worlds in three dimensions. Pictures of far-off lands and strange-looking people, the rocks and canyons of the West and the skyscrapers of the East, the Indians of the Plains and the kings and queens of Europe were all summoned up in the parlour by the magic of the viewing device. As much as they were entertaining, stereos were also educational. In this form of photography the world was reproducible, consumable and fundamentally knowable. Stereos heightened the dramatic elements of the natural world, enhancing their appeal. Viewers could explore the most far-flung destinations, and these sights were contained on the single surface of the card. And the cards were cheap; they sold for $1.50 per dozen, and companies such as E. & H. T. Anthony & Co. in New York and Bradley & Rulofson (later to become Muybridge's publishers) in San Francisco produced and distributed them in the millions. Muybridge made at least 400 stereos of the city. He sold them first through Selleck's Cosmopolitan Gallery and then through other distributors; beginning in 1868, they were stamped 'Helios' and marked 'Entered according to Act of Congress, 1868', indicating that Muybridge was savvy enough to copyright them.

More than mere documents made to entice potential tourists or investors, Muybridge's stereos are the first examples of his attempt to define himself as an artist. He brings to them the sensibility of a British landscape painter, striving for romantic

'An Hour Before Sunset, Bay of San Francisco', 1868, one half of a stereograph in the *Views of San Francisco and Vicinity* series.

effects of shimmering water, sunsets, moonlight and clouds, all familiar to him from the images he marketed during his bookselling career. His photographs fit comfortably within the picturesque tradition found in Baxter's prints and the engravings of Payne's *Pictorial World*, instantly recognizable to, and loved by, a wide audience in both Europe and America.

But Muybridge also looked to photographic models, recognizing the vast potential of a medium that was coming into its own. Photography, which had been lumped in with Musical, Horological and Surgical Instruments at the 1851 Great Exhibition, had been given its own class as a subsection of Machinery at the 1862 London exposition (where Muybridge had exhibited his printing plate and washing machine). And after much discussion among the organizers, jurors and photographers, photographs had been given an autonomous status as objects in their own right, to be displayed separately from the apparatus that made them. As an aspiring photographer, Muybridge would have studied photographs by the masters of the medium. Francis Bedford and Roger Fenton, for example, were two photographers who considered themselves to be artists, and were seen as such by everyone. They apporached their landscape subjects – English valleys, Scottish hills, the ruined abbeys and the cosy cottages – in the British tradition of the Romantic picturesque, framing a distant view with trees to draw in the viewer's eye, capturing rivulets cascading over stones or mountains seen through mist. And he would have seen the work of the well-known Scottish photographer George Washington Wilson, who had depicted the last rays of the sun setting over the lake in his popular *Loch of the Park, Evening*.

Muybridge inevitably scrutinized photographs by Oscar Gustav Rejlander and his colleague Henry Peach Robinson, who were influenced by John Ruskin and the narrative paintings of the Pre-Raphaelites. To make their photographic narratives, Rejlander and Robinson used combination prints, joining multiple negatives to produce a singe print. Rejlander's *Two Ways of Life*, for example, is made up of 40 different negatives of figures – some naked, others dressed in a pastiche of Greek, Roman and biblical robes – printed together to demonstrate the respective choices, one naughty and the other virtuous, made by two brothers. This illustrated morality play was wildly popular and a favourite of Prince Albert. Robinson's *Fading Away* depicts a young girl on the verge of death. As her father gazes through the window at the darkening sky outside – effected by the superimposition of a separate negative – her mother and sister watch over her from either end of her bed.

'Moonlight Effect – The Mission Hills, from Woodward's Gardens', 1869, one half of a stereograph in the *San Francisco* series.

Muybridge emulated Fenton's and Wilson's compositions and effects, and he made them even more pronounced by using the combination techniques of Robinson and Rejlander. Skies were problematic in wet-plate photography because the long exposure needed to achieve a sharp picture would overexpose the sky, turning it into muddy streaks that had to be painted out in indian ink on the negative. Muybridge got around this by overlaying the sky with clouds printed from a separate negative. He would also print figures from one negative into a landscape from another. He was extremely adept at combination printing and other darkroom tricks that would produce the artistic effects he wanted. To achieve the effect of moonlight on water, he shot straight into the sun, creating a round, luminous sphere in an otherwise underexposed negative; for a crescent moon, he would paint over part of the sphere before printing. He would ink out parts of the negative that he felt interfered with his composition, making them disappear from the final print, and he would retouch contours or shapes that he felt should be emphasized.

However, Muybridge didn't rely solely on his darkroom skills. He was also extremely accomplished in the art of pictorial composition. He enhanced the three-dimensional effect of the stereo format, for example, by composing on the diagonal to lead into the distance or from a vantage point that produced a strong contrast between foreground and background. He used the placement of figures creatively, both to give a sense of scale to the picture and to heighten its perspectival depth.

Now confident in his technical skills and with his artistic vision validated by the commercial success of his stereos, Muybridge aspired to capture a larger landscape. He was drawn to the rugged terrain of the American West, joining earlier photographers who had begun to create and shape a national vision by means of their images. Photographs of Western geography and geology – the sublime wilderness, the dense forests of towering sequoias and the geysers, mountains and lakes – conjured a new Eden in the American imagination. They also made visible the idea of Manifest Destiny: the expansion of settlements and railroads across the continent which would bring a new political and social order (and result in the marginalization or disappearance of the native peoples). In 1867 Muybridge decided to strike out for Yosemite.

In the latter part of the nineteenth century Yosemite was almost as difficult to get to as San Francisco had been from New York before the coming of the transcontinental railroad. A contemporary account of the trip describes the obstacles a photographer faced:

> All the traps, and appliances, and chemicals and stores, and provender, have to be got together, and then pack mules secured to carry the load, and drivers to have charge of them. Thus accoutred, the photographer sets out, say, from San Francisco, through hill and vale, across deep fords, over rugged rocks, down steep inclines, and up gorgeous heights, for a journey of one hundred and fifty miles. Several days are thus occupied, and several nights of rest are needed along the road.[2]

Muybridge, ever the adventurer, was not intimidated by such hardships.

It is typical of Muybridge that he chose Yosemite as the site of his first wilderness landscape photographs. In the imagination of Easterners, Yosemite was the mythic heart of the West. Congress had voted to make it a protected area; Abraham Lincoln signed the Yosemite Grant in 1864 at the height of the Civil War. Capturing the glories of Yosemite had made the reputations of other photographers; clearly Muybridge hoped his images would do the same for him. Charles Leander Weed, who was the first to photograph the Valley, had travelled to the area in 1859, and Carleton Watkins had in 1861. For Muybridge, photographing Yosemite was an opportunity to outdo his predecessors, chief of whom was Watkins, whom he came to view as his leading rival.

Born in 1829 in upstate New York, Watkins had first gone West in 1851, travelling via the Isthmus of Panama route with his friend and fellow New Yorker Collis P. Huntington. Huntington, one of the 'Big Four' who would build the Central Pacific Railroad, opened a general store in Sacramento, selling supplies and groceries to mining camps. Watkins worked for him there, but only for a year; in 1852 he moved to San Francisco to clerk in a bookstore on Montgomery Street. He began his photographic career as a camera operator in Robert H. Vance's gallery, a few doors from Muybridge's office on Montgomery, and by 1856 was producing his own ambrotype portraits and landscapes. The earliest were made for the flamboyant John Charles Frémont, a u.s. senator from California in 1850–51 and one of the first larger-than-life Western figures, who in four privately funded expeditions in the 1840s had explored, mapped and even documented in daguerreotypes most of the overland routes to the West needed by the expansion-hungry nation.

Watkins changed studios often; he didn't advertise, opting to sell his pictures through various middlemen and printing according to customer demand. Muybridge was one of those selling Watkins's photographs in 1858. We don't know when the two met, but once they had, they remained in professional contact for years. Watkins was not the consummate businessman that Muybridge was: he did not copyright his photographs until 1867, after more than one publisher had pirated them.

For his first foray into Yosemite in the summer of 1861, Watkins had a camera made large enough to hold 18 × 22 inch (45.7 × 55.9 cm) mammoth plates. He returned with 30 mammoth-plate negatives and 100 stereo negatives. Nothing like the pictures made from these mammoth plates had ever been seen before. Exhibited in December 1862 in Goupil's Art Gallery in New York, they were instrumental in having Congress declare Yosemite an 'inviolate' territory.[3] Watkins returned to Yosemite in the summers of 1865 and 1866 with the California State Geological Survey, taking some of the most admired pictures ever made. He photographed the Mariposa Big Trees, the valleys and the high country with four different cameras: one mammoth, one stereo and two view cameras. Watkins shared the prize for landscape photography at the Paris Exposition of 1867 and in July of that year, as Muybridge was making his first trip into Yosemite Valley, Watkins was sailing up the coast to Portland, Oregon, with Josiah Whitney to photograph the Coast Range mountains, Mount Hood and the Columbia River.

For his 1867 trip to Yosemite, Muybridge took two cameras with him: a stereo and a 5 × 8 inch (14 × 21.6 cm) view camera (though he advertised the prints as being 6 × 8 inches). He seems to have stopped first at the Calaveras Grove of Big Trees and then went on into the Valley, setting up a base at Hutchings' Hotel.[4] Muybridge followed in the steps of Watkins and Weed in expeditions to the base of Upper Yosemite Fall and Illilouette Fall, but he also made it to Glacier Point, Sentinel Dome and Taft Point, venturing much farther than any previous photographer. In order to reach these remote areas, Muybridge had to take tortuously steep trails and carve out the first paths.

He returned with 72 large views and over 100 stereos,[5] and in the spring of 1868 he issued a sales brochure – as he had with his books and engravings – to solicit their sale:

I am now preparing for publication twenty views of our world-renowned Yo-Semite Valley, photographed last year by 'Helios'. For artistic effect, and careful manipulation, they are pronounced by all the best landscape painters and photographers in the city to be the most exquisite photographic views ever produced on this coast, and are marvellous examples of the perfection to which photography can attain in the delineation of sublime and beautiful scenery, as exemplified in our wonderful valley. Upon my list of subscribers for the series – among the names of nearly all our best known connoisseurs and patrons of art – are those of messrs. C. Nahl, Keith, Wandesforde, Norton, Bush, Jewett, Kipps, Denny, Van Vleck, Bloomer, etc., artists; Messrs. Wm Shew, Rulofson, Selleck, A. Nahl, Edouart, White, Vaughan, and other photographers.

The size is most convenient for transmission abroad, for binding, or the portfolio: 6 x 8 inches, mounted on tinted background boards 14 x 18 inches. The price at which they will be issued ($20.00 for the series), placing them within the reach of those having only moderate resources, will probably command for them a sufficiently extensive sale to remunerate me for the great expense of attending their production.

Your obed't Serv't
Edw. J Muybridge
415 Montgomery Street

The pictures were acclaimed in the San Francisco press. On 12 February 1868 the *Bulletin* reviewer compared them favourably to Watkins's earlier work:

Watkins's splendid Yosemite series has long challenged admiration, and has made certain points of the wonderful valley widely known. A new Yosemite series has recently been taken by a photographer of this city, who hides his name under the significant classicism of 'Helios.' These views, 20 or 30 in number, are taken from fresh points, selected with a nice regard to artistic effect, and illustrating the valley and its cliffs and falls more variously than any previous series. There are effects in some of these new views which we have not met before. The plunging movement and half vapory look of cataracts leaping 1,000 or 1,500 feet at a bound, are wonderfully realized. Across some of these falls the arching iris is

seen, colorless but suggestive, like the beauty of a dead face
– the form is there, only the tint and play of nature are lacking.
The cloud effects are caught with capital success. Around and
across some of the granite peaks hang wreaths of vapor, trans-
parent, and full of airy lightness. In one view the sun, the
splendor of his disk veiled by a cloud that yet shows all his
form, is actually made to take his own portrait and mimic in
shadow the 'profuse rays', as our Stoddard calls them, which
he shoots, arrow-like, in toward the dusk. 'Helios' intends to
issue sets of his Yosemite views in portfolio form, and has
already received many subscriptions.

And the *Morning Call*, on 17 February 1868, also praised Muybridge's
artistry: 'Some of the series have just such cloud effects as we see in
nature of oil-painting, but almost never in a photograph.'

In his capacity as former Board Director of the Mercantile Library,
Muybridge presented the organization with a few of the prints,
together with personal note:

> Some of the members of your board I know to possess consider-
> able discrimination and a very refined taste in artistic matters,
> I shall therefore be pleased to receive and [*sic*] expression of the
> board's opinion respecting the merits of the prints.
>   Your worthy Ex-President whom I believe to be considerable
> of a connoisseur expressed a desire to have them framed and
> placed in some desirable place in the new building, should
> this be concurred in by the rest of the board I shall feel highly
> flattered. I am, Gentlemen,
>   Your Obd't Serv't
>   (E. J. Muybridge)

He also sent 125 prints to the editor of the *Philadelphia Photographer*, which in April 1868 published the commendation of the

Photographic Society of Pennsylvania: 'That this Society takes great pleasure in attesting their high appreciation of the artistic skill in the selection of these views, and the eminent talent evinced in their photographic reproduction.'

The journal's notice was a critical one: Philadelphia could rightly be called the birthplace of American landscape photography. The Philadelphia photographer John Moran would work with William Henry Jackson on the Hayden Survey of the West in 1870. Another native, Coleman Sellers, who would play an important role in Muybridge's life twenty years later by funding Muybridge's work at the University of Pennsylvania, had popularized the 1863 globe lens specifically for landscape photography. The journal's editor, Edward L. Wilson, featured landscape prominently in almost every issue and even prescribed the requisite elements of a desirable landscape image, including motionless trees and reflections in water.[6] When Wilson tipped in five of Muybridge's prints in the November 1869 issue and compared the photographer to the 'great [George Washington] Wilson, of Scotland', Muybridge's reputation was secured.

Eighteen of Muybridge's tipped-in albumen prints also made their way into one of the earliest guidebooks for the region, John Hittell's *Yosemite: Its Wonders and its Beauties* (San Francisco, H. H. Bancroft and Company, 1868). In true entrepreneurial spirit, Muybridge compiled his reviews into an ad placed in the endpapers of the book:

EDW. J. MUYBRIDGE

Has now made for sale the most comprehensive and beautiful
series of Views, illustrating the wonderful
SCENERY OF THE YOSEMITE VALLEY
ever executed. They comprise 250 Views of the various Falls,
Precipices, and most picturesque and interesting
points of sight fit the valley.

100, 6 x 8 inches, mounted on India tinted boards, 14 x 18 inches,
price, $1.25 each, or $1 each, in quantities of 20 and upwards.
160 Views for the Stereoscope, price $4.50 per dozen.
Card-size, for the album, $2.50.
All of these can be had unmounted, for the convenience of those
wishing to forward them by mail. A complete series of the same,
various sizes, illustrating the most noted Mammoth Trees in the
State. These views are by 'HELIOS', and are justly celebrated as
being the most artistic and remarkable photographs ever
produced on this coast. [See criticisms.]
Also preparing for publication, a complete series of
SAN FRANCISCO VIEWS
and a series illustrating *MINING SCENES*,
and the principal Places of interest on the Coast.

The ad concluded with several 'Opinions of the Press', excerpts
from gushing reviews of the work that had appeared in the
Philadelphia Photographer, Evening Bulletin, Alta California and
Morning Call.

In his Yosemite pictures Muybridge was able to meld his experience
with the stereo format and his darkroom skills to the lessons he
had learned from Fenton and other landscape photographers. He
often composed his pictures to emphasize depth, sometimes using
a reflecting sheet of water to lead the eye through the middle and
background of the scene. He used trees to frame and centre motifs
such as waterfalls. He heavily retouched many of the pictures, eliminating what he felt were intrusions or sharpening outlines. And
although he still printed in clouds in some pictures, he also devised
a groundbreaking method for overcoming the technical limitations
of his process. His 'sky shade', which he patented in 1869, held back
the amount of light reaching the sky part of the negative while the
landscape area was fully exposed. In this way, he could capture the

actual clouds in the sky and control the mood of the pictures, almost as if he were double printing the image right in the camera.[7]

Muybridge's depictions of clouds were especially appealing to novelist Helen Hunt Jackson. Her 1884 masterwork *Ramona*, recounting the adventures of a half-native, half-Scottish orphan, aimed to do for Indian rights what Harriet Beecher Stowe's *Uncle Tom's Cabin* had done for the abolitionist cause. Viewing the pictures in Muybridge's studio, Hunt wrote that he was 'an artist by nature', whose photographs 'have composition' as well as 'such unity, such effect, such vitality . . . in comparison with the average photograph, which has been made hap-hazard, to cover so many square feet and take in all that happened to be there.' Hunt picked out the skies in his Yosemite pictures for special praise. 'Mr Muybridge's pictures have another peculiarity, which of itself would mark them superior to others. The skies are always most exquisitely rendered. His cloud photographs alone fill a volume; and many of them remind one vividly of Turner's studies of skies. The contrast between a photographed landscape, with a true sky added, and one with the usual ghastly, lifeless, pallid, stippled sky is something which it is impossible to overstate.'[8]

In another strategy that would become almost a trademark, Muybridge included himself in some of his pictures. In *Charon at the Ferry*, for example, Yosemite's Merced River becomes the River Styx and Muybridge poses as the mythic ferryman who transports the souls of the dead across the water to Hades. Many of his pictures focus on water, both the reflecting lake and the rushing waterfalls. And although the long exposures rendered the falls as flat white sheets, Muybridge's ability to evoke the movement of water was remarked upon. In the *Daily Alta California* of 17 February 1868, the reporter comments on the rainbow that Muybridge captured on the spray of the Nevada Fall and claims that 'the effect of falling water shown in a photograph of the base of the Lower Yosemite Fall, is also very wonderful, and cannot be sufficiently admired.'

Muybridge's Yosemite photographs were so highly regarded because they exemplified the aesthetic sensibility created by British painters and then adopted by American landscape artists such as Frederic Church, John Moran and Albert Bierstadt – all of whose works, as well as those of local painters and engravers, had been shown since 1865 in San Francisco's California Art Union. Muybridge filtered the Western landscape through European eyes. His photographs, in their artistic effects and their reliance on darkroom techniques to render them, are different from the Western landscapes of Watkins and other contemporary Americans such as Timothy O'Sullivan and William H. Jackson, whose photographs

Charon at the Ferry, 1867.

of the wilderness were produced as part of government surveys. Watkins photographed Yosemite for Josiah Whitney; O'Sullivan worked for Clarence King's 1867–9 survey of the Fortieth Parallel following the path of the nearly completed railroad; and Jackson travelled with Ferdinand Hayden's nearly decade-long survey of the Rocky Mountains beginning in the 1870s. All were employed to record the topography of the area, to photograph the geological formations, to picture the best sites through which to lay tracks for the transcontinental railroad and to assess the natural resources that could be tapped by the homesteader and the tourist. They worked alongside geologists and engineers – scientists whose interests lay in documenting the unknown territory. The stereos of photographers such as Watkins, O'Sullivan and Jackson were often copyrighted and captioned by the publisher or survey leader. They were photographers in the service of science. Muybridge operated from within a very different mindset: he was out to make art in the tradition of the picturesque landscape. As noted previously, he controlled both the copyright and the description of his images from early in his career.

Muybridge's ad in Hitell's *Yosemite* book concludes with his call for new work:

> HELIOS is prepared to accept commissions to photograph Private Residences, Ranches, Mills, Views, Animals, Ships, etc., anywhere in the city, or any portion of the Pacific Coast.
> Architects', Surveyors' and Engineers' Drawings copied mathamatically [*sic*] correct.
> Photographic copies of Paintings and Works of Art.

Illustrating government survey commissions was one of the best ways for wet-plate photographers to earn a steady income. Although Muybridge's atmospheric and artistic production might not appeal to the military man, engineer or geologist who usually led such projects, his documentation of city architectural landmarks such as the Masonic temple showcased his technical expertise. In the summer of 1868, as he was finishing the publication of his Yosemite photographs, Muybridge was commissioned by the government to accompany General Henry Wager Halleck on his tour of the 'Military Posts and the Harbors of Alaska'. Halleck, one of the principal authors of the California state constitution, had been General in Chief of the u.s. Army during the Civil War, before the more aggressive Ulysses S. Grant was promoted over him in 1864. Halleck was an intellectual and a scholar – his nickname 'old brains' went hand in hand with his reputation for being dry and distant – and his postwar assignment as military director of the Pacific was a form of professional exile. The object of his survey was generally perceived as equally marginal. A year earlier, under the direction of Secretary of State William H. Steward, the United States had bought Alaska from Russia for $7,200,000.00, and many critics of the purchase shared the opinion expressed by Horace Greeley, the journalist who coined the phrase 'Go West, young man':

> [Alaska] contained nothing of value but furbearing animals, and these had been hunted until they were nearly extinct. Except for the Aleutian Islands and a narrow strip of land extending along the southern coast the country would be not worth taking as a gift . . . Unless gold were found in the country much time would elapse before it would be blessed with Hoe printing presses, Methodist chapels and a metropolitan police. It was 'a frozen wilderness.'[9]

But other accounts had suggested that the territory was more than just fur and natives; Halleck's journey with Muybridge was commissioned in order to gather evidence that would help persuade the public that 'Seward's folly' was not a folly at all.

On 29 July, fifteen days after Congress finally approved the purchase, Muybridge and Halleck set sail on the steamer *Pacific*. Muybridge photographed the British Columbian coastal towns of Victoria and Nanaimo (one of the reasons for the purchase of Alaska was to keep the British from buying it) and then took pictures as they passed through the channels and islands of the Queen Charlottes, over the open water, to the forts at Tongass, Wrangell and finally Sitka, where they arrived on 18 August. Muybridge's pictures of Sitka – formerly called Archangel – included not only the forts and civilian buildings, the Russian Orthodox church and its priests, but also several groups of native Tlingit people. His images of the Tlingit are typical of mid-nineteenth-century photographs of non-Europeans that followed the tradition of scientific illustrations accompanying accounts of expeditions and voyages, such as Captain Cook's to the South Seas. Muybridge would have seen such illustrations in the books he sold; he would also have seen the photographs recording human geography at the 1862 London exhibition. Like the photographers who brought back images of the peoples of China, the South Pacific, the Middle East and Africa, Muybridge's pictures, in which he posed the Tlingit frontally and photographed them from a distance, emphasize the race and class differences between himself – and by extension, the viewer – and his subjects. We don't know if they were lured by money to pose, were tricked or were complicit in the experience, but they stare directly at the camera with vacant and bewildered expressions. Like a mug shot or a passport picture, their portrayal invites an anthropological reading of their exotic 'otherness'. Muybridge's numerous depictions, each titled 'Group of Indians', include chiefs in all their finery and a group seated under a totem. They are among the very first pictures of Alaskan natives and would have fuelled the almost insatiable curiosity on the part of tourists and colonizers alike about physical difference. The Tlingit are not identified by name; they are centred in the frame, posed against their building or camp, and as such they take on the role of specimens, unconnected to any social or human context but part of a 'primitive' culture.

Although opposition to the purchase of Alaska would completely disappear only with the Klondike Gold Strike in 1896, Muybridge's pictures did help convey to Americans the value of the new territory. On 9 October 1868, a note in the *Bulletin* applauded the exhibition of two pictures, one of Sitka and the other of Fort Wrangle, painted from Muybridge's photographs:

> Both these Alaska views are taken by Mr Muygridge [*sic*] during a recent trip to our new territory. California photographers are

'Group of Indians', 1868, one half of a stereograph in the *Alaska* series.

doing a good service in many ways by their enterprise in land-scape work, which is making familiar in the parlors of the nation some of the finest scenery in the least explored parts of the Union. Watkins lately photographed the mountain and river scenery of Oregon and Washington; and now Muygridge brings us Alaska in a portfolio of sun pictures that give us a very favorable opinion of Greeley's 'Walrussia.'[10]

In a letter of 13 October 1868 Halleck acknowledged Muybridge's work as giving 'a more correct idea of Alaska and its scenery and vegetation than can be obtained from any written description of that country'.[11] Seward himself praised the photographs' artistic excellence and, according to a notice in the *Alaska Herald*, the pictures were still selling well four years after Muybridge took them.[12]

Back in San Francisco, on 21 October Muybridge documented the ruins caused by the most severe earthquake the city had ever experienced. Working more in the fashion of a photojournalist than an artist, he captured images of the tilted and crumbling buildings and the crowds that had come to see them. A month later he photographed the steamships *Colorado* and *Golden City*, the latter in the new dry dock that had been built at Hunter's Point. These photographs, those of the earthquake and Muybridge's Alaska series – produced as both stereos and large mounted views – were sold in both stores and galleries. The diversity of these locations reflects the broad scope of Muybridge's photographic practice, its marketability and his talent for self-promotion. At 38 years of age, he now fashioned himself an official government photographer: 'Director of photographic surveys on the Pacific Coast.' On the back of his stereo cards he advertised 'the most artistic and comprehensive series of Pacific Coast, Yosemite, and Mammoth Tree Views, ever published, of various sizes, adapted for framing, the stereoscope and the album'.[13] All the advertising paid off. Muybridge expanded his sales through the London

Stereoscopic Company in New York. He continued to work with the army, documenting the forts and soldiers at Fort Point, Point San Jose, Black Point and the island of Alcatraz; this work would lead to a commission to photograph the lighthouses along the Pacific coast in 1871. He successfully marketed his views in a number of series, including 70 stereos that were part of a *Pacific Coast Series* and one devoted to the Vancouver and Farallon Islands, once more competing with Watkins, who was publishing his *Watkins' Pacific Coast Views* and covering much of the same ground.

In the spring of 1869 the transcontinental railroad was completed. This joining of the two coasts would shape the future of America and transform the city of San Francisco. The 'golden spike' was driven at Promontory Summit, Utah, on 10 May 1869, physically joining the Union Pacific company's thousand miles of track from Omaha to the Central Pacific company's line from Sacramento and symbolically binding one coast of the nation to the other with iron bands. At 2:47 pm, Leland Stanford, former governor of California and president of the Central Pacific Railroad, delivered the blow with a silver hammer made especially for the ceremony. A telegraph wire attached to the hammer and connected to a line that ran along the tracks transmitted Stanford's gesture to every telegraph station in the country. The 'victory over space, the elements, and the stupendous mountain barriers separating San Francisco from the world' was simultaneously signalled from San Francisco to New York.[14]

The idea for a transcontinental railroad, which would establish direct access to Eastern markets and capital and a gateway to Asia from the West, predated the annexation of California in 1848. Slave and non-slave states could not agree upon a southern route, so one following the stagecoach lines across the desert and through the mountains of the Sierra Nevada was chosen. It took many years to solve the problems that arose from the route's passage through such inhospitable terrain, which was also subject to extremes of summer heat and winter snow. A government survey begun under then Secretary of War Jefferson Davis in 1853 was completed in 1855. The Pacific Railroad Act, signed into law by Abraham Lincoln on 1 July 1862, provided the financing. It gave a mortgage to two corporations, the Central Pacific Railroad (CPRR) company in the West and the Union Pacific Railroad (UPRR) in the East, and granted each a 200-foot (61-metre) strip of land on both sides of the right of way and 64,000 acres in return for each mile of track they completed. The CPRR and the UPRR also received loans in government bonds for each mile constructed to be paid back in transportation and services to the government. In effect, the government was giving the corporations a license to print money.

The CPRR had been incorporated in Sacramento on 28 June 1861 with a capital stock of $8,500,000 – 85,000 shares at $100 each. The initial subscriptions were made by the men who would become known as the 'Big Four': the company's president Leland Stanford; its vice-president (Watkins's patron) Collis Huntington; its secretary-treasurer Mark Hopkins, Huntington's business partner in hardware wholesale; and its lawyer E. B. Crocker, whose brother Charles, a dry-goods merchant, was a director. The Big Four were the original robber barons: through their shares in the railroad, construction contracts, government loans, land grants and railroad fees – many acquired by bribery, coercion and undue influence – they would become the wealthiest men in the West. In one way or another, they would all come to exert an important influence on Muybridge's life. Stanford in particular would be instrumental in propelling Muybridge onto the world stage.

Stanford was, like Huntington and Crocker, an Easterner. Born in 1824 in what is now the town of Colonie, New York, Stanford came to Sacramento during the Gold Rush to sell groceries and mining supplies. He was a political man, one of the founders in March 1856 of the Republican Party of California. Strongly anti-slavery, the party presented John Frémont as their first (unsuccessful) presidential candidate. In 1859 Stanford ran unsuccessfully for

'Interior of Snow Sheds, Western Summit, Sierra Nevada Mountains', 1869, one half of a stereograph in the *Central Pacific Railroad* series.

governor. The election of the Republican Abraham Lincoln as president and the ensuing Civil War brought the California Republicans increased power. Stanford was elected governor in 1861 and served until 1863.

Stanford's belief in the railroad was part of his faith in Union victory. When that victory came, delivering a country now free from slavery and a West wide open to rapid development, the railroad became a reality and Stanford a Croesus. His Golden Spike represented a triumph over all risks and barriers to expansion: the hostile natives; the unknown geology, flora and fauna; the extreme climates, dangerous avalanches and limited water sources. All had been eliminated, confined, tamed or surveyed.

One of the engineering marvels of the nineteenth century, the transcontinental railroad was the technological embodiment of Manifest Destiny, which presumed a divine sanction for American expansion. It developed the economy of the West even as it consumed its natural resources; it destroyed the life and culture of the native peoples; and it standardized time across the continent, synchronizing Eastern and Western clocks to the railroad and ending thousands of years of human activity unregulated by mechanically measured global time.

Photographers, with their assistants, cameras, plates and chemicals, followed every mile of the work joining East and West. Andrew J. Russell was assigned to document construction of the Union Pacific while Alfred A. Hart, a painter turned photographer, was hired by the CPRR to follow its construction from 1864 until its completion.[15] Hart was on the train that brought Stanford from Sacramento to Promontory Summit; Russell's picture of the driving of the last spike is the most famous record of the occasion. Their pictures documented the scale of the terrain, the settlements and native peoples as well as the stupendous feats of engineering through the mountains that brought the railroad into being. But these pictures alone were not enough to meet the high demand for depictions of the railroad's progress. And both Muybridge and Watkins, who, when Hart's patron Crocker had a stroke a few months later, would become the official photographer for the CPRR, joined other photographers in the effort to document this history in the making.

As Helios, Muybridge published two series, one of the Central Pacific Railroad and the other of the Union Pacific. They mark his travels across California, Nevada and Utah to end at the 'thousand mile tree' marking the distance from Omaha, the beginning point of the Union Pacific. They include views of the mountains and canyons,

'Shoshone Indians at Corinne', Utah, 1869, one half of a stereograph in the *Central Pacific Railroad* series.

lakes and valleys along the route and the engineering feats that had conquered the terrain – the cuts and tunnels dynamited through the mountains, the trestle bridges and the extraordinary snow sheds that kept the railroad free of the fifty-foot drifts that piled up during the winter in the Sierras. Muybridge used many of his standard effects, including moonlight and fog, and he found the tunnels and snow sheds to be perfect for emphasizing the stereo's deep space. He photographed from inside these structures as if they were vast cathedrals framing the wide vistas beyond or stretching into a dark infinity. In his images of the lakes and rivers traversed by the railroad, he often placed a figure in the middle of the frame, or just slightly off centre, to establish both the scale of the landscape and the foreground of the picture. The faces of these figures are in shadow as befits their status as mere markers in the picture. But along the way he also photographed people as subjects – a group of labourers on a trestle, for example, and in Corinne, Utah, five Shoshone natives. He posed them in typical 'specimen' fashion, as he had done with the Tlingit, in the centre of the frame gazing directly into the camera. One of them, however, holds a bow and arrow; his arm is drawn back and the arrow, about to be loosed, is aimed directly at the photographer. This threatening gesture must have been Muybridge's idea for he photographed the same warrior again in a more peaceable pose, this time standing in front of a tepee in his camp at the foot of the Wasatch Mountains.

Both Watkins and Muybridge moved to new galleries in the spring of 1869 to capitalize on the influx of tourists about to descend on the city. Probably financed by Collis Huntington, Watkins moved from his Yo-Semite Gallery at 425 Montgomery Street to a larger space at 429, next to the gallery of publishers Bradley & Rolufson. Muybridge meanwhile, left Selleck's gallery at 415 Montgomery to sell his pictures through Nahl's at 121, while maintaining two other spaces, his own studio at 111 Montgomery and a sales booth at Woodward's Gardens. Selleck and Muybridge remained friends, but Nahl's gallery was a better fit for Muybridge. Its principal, Charles Nahl, was an artist, a well-established California genre and portrait painter whose most popular picture, *Sunday Morning in the Mines* (1872), a nostalgic look at the Sierra Nevada miners at the beginning of the Gold Rush, was commissioned by Judge E. B. Crocker. (Miners were a popular subject; Muybridge had announced his own mining scenes for publication in May 1868.) It was Nahl who had decorated the membership certificates sold for the 1856 vigilante committee organized after the assassination of James King of William.[16] And Nahl was the founder of the Olympic

Club, the first athletic club in the United States, whose star athletes would be among the subjects of Muybridge's first stop-action photographs in 1879. Nahl's close association with the art world and with Crocker, one of the 'Big Four', provided a greater advantage to the photographer than anything Selleck could offer.

Muybridge would stay with Nahl for only two years. But during that time his output was prodigious both in scope and in the way he exploited his medium. He made a series that tracked the building of the San Francisco Mint, each image marking a phase of its construction as it progressed over time from a hole in the ground to a stolid edifice. His series depicting Great Geyser Springs and Calistoga Springs advertised these tourist destinations in the manner of modern travel brochures. We get a glimpse of how Muybridge's imagination worked in the figure of a devil that he printed into one image and his literary tastes in the captioning of the silhouettes of three women as 'The Witches Caldron – Macbeth, Act IV scene I.' And he began to photograph in Woodward's Gardens where, for the first time, he featured a model, a young girl who worked at Nahl's as a retoucher named Flora Shallcross Stone.

3

The Wild Wild West

Woodward's Gardens was one of the most popular leisure spots in San Francisco in the nineteenth century, containing, among other attractions, the largest zoo on the West Coast, an amusement park, four museums and an art gallery. It had been created by wealthy San Francisco hotel owner Robert B. Woodward, who in 1866 extended his own estate to include exotic plants, a skating rink, hot-air balloon rides and a 'Rotary boat' that sailed like a merry-go-round along a track around a large circular pond. This 'Barnum of the West', as Woodward came to be known, also displayed stuffed animals and human curiosities: Japanese acrobats, circus freaks, tribes of American Indians, Sandwich Islanders and the famous Chinese giant Chang Woo Gow.

Both tourists and locals who visited the Gardens could buy pictorial souvenirs at Muybridge's shop just inside the entrance. There he sold his stereo pictures of the artworks on view, such as the statue personifying *California* by Hiram Powers, the renowned sculptor of the Crystal Palace's *The Greek Slave*, together with the other exotic nude subjects – *Indian Girl*, *Baccante* and *Pandora* – surrounded by copies of world-famous paintings. In one of these photographs, Muybridge positioned himself as the very image of the cultured gentleman he saw himself to be, sitting among the paintings and sculptures. To accommodate the long exposure time he has bowed his head and lowered his eyes in order to remain still. In another image, he photographs himself in a reflection taking a

'Art Gallery at Woodward's Gardens', 1870, one half of a stereograph in the *San Francisco* series.

photograph, demonstrating his skill with the camera. In still other pictures taken at the Gardens, he records the entertainments with his own form of visual spectacle. His photographs of Chang Woo Gow emphasize the effect of the man by capturing the expressions on the faces of the crowds who gaze up at the towering figure. He also photographed Chang next to his diminutive wife as well as his wife alone, but in a carte-de-visite format.

In this Woodward Gardens series, published in September 1870, Muybridge includes figures in new ways. One series of stereos can be read as a sequence following two men as they wander through the park. Another features a young woman with plump cheeks,

'Animals at Woodward's Gardens' (Flora), 1870, one half of a stereograph in the *Views of the Pacific Coast* series.

long oval ears and a prominent nose; her hair is drawn back and up into a cascade of curls; a hat tilts over her forehead. This is Flora, Muybridge's future wife. At least three pictures show her with taxidermy: in one she is kneeling to caress a tiger and in another she is seated on the grass among a group of deer, with a fawn on her lap. Another photograph shows her from the back sitting on a small fence on the left side of the picture, her face turned toward the camera, her right arm holding a small parasol. She wears different clothes in these pictures; they were not all taken on the same day.

In her own way, Flora was as much of a risk-taker as Muybridge was. Born in 1851, she was a little more than half his age when they

'Scene at Woodward's Gardens' (Flora), one half of a stereograph, 1870.

met. Orphaned as a child, she had made the harsh journey west with a certain uncle 'Stump', a steamboat captain who had placed her with an aunt named Downs. At sixteen she married Lucius Stone, a San Francisco saddle maker and wholesaler whom she divorced in 1870 on grounds of cruelty. Left to support herself, she worked as a 'saleswoman in a fancy goods store on Kearny street',[1] and then as a photographic retoucher both at Nahl's and at Bradley and Rulofson's.

Flora seems not to have been bothered by the disparity in their ages. Muybridge was prosperous and he was an established figure in both the business and cultural worlds of the city. For someone like her, who had grown up an impoverished orphan, he represented the path to social acceptance and financial security. On his part, Muybridge cared deeply for her. She was plump, pretty and young. But he cared more for his photography. He often left her alone, assuming, perhaps, that she was made from the same mould as the women he knew best, his mother and grandmother: models of strong, morally upright wives and mothers.

Flora and Muybridge married on 20 May 1871. During the months leading up to their wedding, 'Helios' still kept up a strenuous travel schedule. Between the middle of March and the end of April, he worked on another government commission, this time for the United States Light House Board.

In exchange for twenty dollars per day, which, Muybridge wrote, would cover 'safe transportation for myself and apparatus, and remuneration for my time, chemicals and use of apparatus', he agreed to provide two prints of 'all the Light Houses upon this coast, and such further views as you may direct of other points without extra charge'.[2] Muybridge approached this project as a documentary commission and at times inscribed the backs of his pictures with explanations of the eccentric viewpoints needed to accurately portray the buildings and their setting. That did not prevent him, however, from making pictures of ethereal beauty where the lighthouse sits on a hill over a raging ocean, or its lights are perceived dimly through an all-encompassing fog.

Immediately after his marriage, Muybridge stayed relatively close to home for a time, working on a supply of saleable images of the particular characteristics of the West Coast. He produced one of the earliest photographic studies of the Chinese who in waves of immigration – the most recent being the unskilled 'coolie' labour hired to build the railroad – made up 5 per cent of San Francisco's population. Although Chinese immigrants had earlier been admired for their industriousness and frugality, by the 1860s they were viewed with increasing suspicion and fear. And in 1870, the year before Muybridge photographed them, the u.s. government passed the Naturalization Act restricting immigration to 'white persons and persons of African descent'. The law, reiterated more strongly by the passing of the Chinese Exclusion Act in 1882, effectively prohibited the entry of any new Asian immigrants and made those already in America ineligible for citizenship. The act would not be abolished until 1943.

In parallel with his ethnographic descriptions of the Chinese, Muybridge published a series of 'Indians of the West Coast' and, in the late summer of 1871, he agreed to a second commissioned trip to photograph the coastal lighthouses. This time he included the new lighthouse at Point Reyes and one on South Farallon Island. A few years earlier, in 1868, Watkins had photographed the Farallon Islands, a group of windswept uninhabited rocks 30 miles (50 km) off San Francisco. So it is no surprise to find Muybridge staying on to make a series on the islands, 'some of the most rugged, singular and interesting scenery upon the coast'.[3]

When he returned from that trip, Muybridge almost immediately set out again, this time travelling 50 miles (80 km) north of the city to Sonoma to make one of the earliest photo essays. Made at the Buena Vista Winery, one of the oldest in the state and the first to have stone cellars, *A Vintage in California* follows the winemaking process from the planting of the vines to the bottling of the vintage. Robert C. Johnson, who had crossed paths with Muybridge in Paris in 1862, was a member of the winery's board and proffered the invitation. Muybridge photographed the vineyard labourers from afar so that they seem to merge with the very land they worked. His artistic depiction of these scenes was reminiscent of contemporaneous European paintings of peasant labour. Helen Hunt Jackson connected them to Dutch still-lifes and to the depictions of French peasants by the Barbizon School painter Jean-Françoise Millet, whose *Angelus* (1857–9) and *The Gleaners* (1857) would have been familiar to her readers

'Buena Vista Vineyard, Sonoma – Disgorging the Sediment and re-corking Sparkling Wine', 1871–2, one half of a stereograph in the series *A Vintage in California*.

through engravings. Looking at Muybridge's Buena Vista series in 1872, she wrote:

> Mr Muybridge has a series of eight pictures illustrative of the California vintage, all of which are exquisitely beautiful, and any one of which, painted in true color simply from the photograph as it stands, would seem to be a picture from a master's hand. One of the first pictures in the series, representing the first breaking of the soil for the vineyard, is as perfect a Millet as could be imagined. The soft tender distance, outlined by low

mountain ranges; a winding road, losing itself in a wood; a bare and stricken tree on the right of the foreground; and in the centre a solitary man, ploughing the ground. Next comes the same scene, with the young vines just starting. The owner is sitting on a bank in the foreground, looking off dreamily over his vineyard. Then there are two pictures representing the cutting of the grapes and the piling of them into the baskets and the wagons. The grouping of the vintagers in these is exquisite. Then there is a picture of the storehouses and the ranges of casks; all so judiciously selected and placed that it might be a photograph from some old painting of still life in Meran. The last picture of all is of the corking the bottles. Only a group of workmen, under an open shed, corking wine-bottles; but every accessory is so artistically thrown in that the whole scene reminds one of Teniers.[4]

Back in San Francisco in February, Muybridge again photographed the phases of a building as it underwent construction, this time the new City Hall and its law courts. His desire to illustrate each phase of construction testifies to a certain civic pride in the municipal and – as in the case of the Mint – federal buildings that were now going up all over San Francisco; but it also suggests his interest in the depiction of change over time. This interest would soon become the main focus of his work.

All through August and early September 1870, Muybridge had advertised that Helios was prepared to 'photograph private residences, animals, or views in the city or any part of the coast'. In 1871 the ads had fallen off, and by 1872 they had disappeared altogether: Helios was disappearing into the shadows and Muybridge, under the patronage of Leland Stanford, was coming into the light. In April 1872 Muybridge travelled to Sacramento to solicit subscribers for a new Yosemite project. There he met Stanford for the first time, and the railroad tycoon invited Muybridge to photograph his recently built mansion. The photographer's reputation alone would certainly have merited the commission, or Stanford might have been aware of Muybridge's advertisement. On the other hand, Muybridge's association with Nahl, and Nahl's connection to Stanford's partner Crocker, is an equally likely source of the invitation.

Muybridge made 23 negatives of Stanford's house at Eighth and N. Streets in Sacramento: different views of the exterior from close up and farther away, the front entrance, the foyer and then each room of the interior in turn. In some of the interiors, Muybridge photographed the family sitting informally; one taken in the billiards room shows Stanford's wife, Jane, and her sister Mary Lathrop enjoying a game while Leland Stanford Junior, then a tiny tot, exchanges glances with his mother. The decoration of the house, done by Jane, is very much in the style of the *belle époque*: heavy furniture and lots of weighty, velvet drapery. Yet, by repeatedly filling them with the Stanford women – in addition to his wife and sister-in-law, both Leland's mother and mother-in-law lived in the house – Muybridge managed to make the house more than just a series of lavishly furnished, cavernous rooms.

Muybridge also photographed Stanford's carriage horses at Sacramento's Agricultural Park racetrack. Made immensely wealthy by his rail investments, Stanford had become a horse connoisseur, partly in response to his doctor's orders. Apparently suffering from nervous exhaustion from the stress of railroad building, he had been ordered to go on a vacation but instead, as he later recounted, he 'bought a little horse, that turned out to be remarkably fast, and it was in the using of it that I became interested in the study of the horse and its actions'.[5]

That little horse, called 'Charley', began his life as a cart-horse; but it soon became obvious to his original owner, a grocer, that the animal was built for speed. In 1870, after Stanford saw 'Charley' race, he bought him for $4,000 in gold, renamed him 'Occident' and proceeded to train him. Never one to do anything by halves, Stanford focused on the latest and most scientific methods for understanding the motions of the horse and in particular for solving the 'unsupported transit' controversy: did the horse have all four legs off the ground at one point in the trot or gallop, or did it not? Stanford was not alone in wanting to know the answer to this and other questions concerning equine locomotion. The animal was critical to transportation, travel, recreation, social status and war. But its movements were too swift and complex ever to be grasped by the naked eye.

The numerous theories that had been posited as to how the animal actually moved had prompted a number of experiments. In one, each hoof of a horse was shod differently so that it would be possible to distinguish by ear the order of the hooves as they

Leland Stanford Jr, Jane Stanford and Mary Lathrop at the Sacramento Stanford Residence, 1872.

struck the ground. In another, a distinctly shaped shoe was fitted to each hoof to make prints in sand. In 1870, the French physiologist Étienne-Jules Marey, whose studies would be important to Stanford's research, had begun to trace the sequence of a horse's gait by graphs. His system translated each footfall as part of a sinuous curve. In the spring of 1872, just as Marey was preparing to publish these curves along with drawings of the horse in the positions indicated by them, Stanford asked Muybridge to photograph 'Occident'.

The ultimate success of Muybridge's instantaneous images of 'Occident' and Stanford's other horses made the photographer world famous; it also led to a lawsuit between the two men over who had rights to publication of the photographs. The sour denouement of their collaboration might explain the multiple accounts of how the work originated.

Muybridge himself gave at least three versions, first crediting Stanford alone with the idea, claiming that he was 'perfectly amazed at the boldness and originality of the proposition' and uncertain at first if it could be carried out.[6] In 1879 he declared, 'I have not, nor do not claim any credit for these photographs: whatever praise others may have felt proper to award, has been entirely unsolicited and to which Governor Leland Stanford is entitled much more than I. He originally suggested the idea.'[7] But in 1883, at a talk at Philadelphia's Franklin Institute, Muybridge gave the impression that the idea was not Stanford's alone:

Having devoted much attention in California to experiments in instantaneous photography, I, in 1872, at the suggestion of the editor of a San Francisco newspaper, obtained a few photo-graphic impressions of a horse during a fast trot. At this time much controversy prevailed among experienced horsemen as to whether all the feet of a horse while trotting were entirely clear of the ground at the same instant of time. A few experiments made in that year proved a fact which should have been self-evident.[8]

The editor in question is generally acknowledged to be Frank McCrellish of the San Francisco *Alta California* and it is from a first-hand account in the 7 April 1873 issue of the paper that we have the only reliable proof that any photographs were ever taken, since none have survived. The account, however, describes a particular success that could only have occurred that year, and not in 1872 when Muybridge first started working for Stanford:

All the sheets in the neighbourhoods of the stable were procured to make a white ground to reflect the object and 'Occident' was after a while trained to go over the white cloth without flinching: then came the question how could an impression be transfixed of a body moving at the rate of thirty-eight feet to the second. The first experiment of opening and closing the camera on the first day left no result; the second day, with increased velocity in opening and closing, a shadow was caught. On the third day, Mr Muybridge, having studied the matter thoroughly, contrived to have two boards slip past each other by touching a spring and in so doing to leave an eighth of an inch opening for the five-hundredth part of a second, as the horse passed, and by an arrangement of double lenses, crossed, secured a negative that shows 'Occident' in full motion – a perfect likeness of the celebrated horse. The space of time was so small that the spokes of the sulky were caught as if they were not in motion. This is considered a great triumph as a curiosity in photography – a horse's picture taken while going thirty-eight feet in a second.

Muybridge's final account, written in 1899, attributes the initiative to himself:

In the spring of the year 1872, while the author was directing the photographic surveys of the United States Government on the Pacific Coast, there was revived in the city of San Francisco a controversy in regard to animal locomotion . . . The principal subject of dispute was the possibility of a horse, while trotting – even at the height of his speed – having all four of his feet, at any portion of his stride, simultaneously free from contact with the ground. The attention of the author was directed to this controversy, and he immediately resolved to attempt its settlement.[9]

Despite these conflicting stories, it is clear that Muybridge must have made enough progress in 1872 for Stanford to invite him back to try again a year later.

In between his two attempts at photographing 'Occident', Muybridge made his second trip to Yosemite. The prospectus to potential subscribers he published from Nahl's studio in May 1872 entitled each buyer to select 'forty pictures 18 x 22 inches of Yosemite' for $100. This was Muybridge's first work with a mammoth-plate camera and he felt confident in his ability to achieve the desired results. Muybridge produced his prospectus with an eye to Watkins's success. Encouraged by the fact that 'although many carefully executed large-size photographs of our scenery have already been published', Muybridge writes, 'the wonderful improvement in the science of photographic manipulation, and a judicious selection of points of view, with an aim at the highest artistic treatment the subject affords, will result in a more complete realization than has hitherto been accomplished'.[10]

Toward the end of June, Muybridge left Flora again and set out for Yosemite with packers, mules and probably two assistants, though we only know the name of one, Robert Towne. Going into the park, his 'long line of pack-mules' met Helen Hunt Jackson on her way out. As Hunt's party drew aside to let the mules pass, she noted that they

were loaded with a photographer's apparatus, lenses, plates, camera, carefully packed boxes of chemicals. Some of these parcels we had seen while in process of preparation in San Francisco. Their owner, Mr Muybridge, has just established himself in the valley for the summer, for the purpose of taking a series of views, larger and more perfect than any heretofore attempted.[11]

As he had done in 1867, Muybridge travelled to parts of Yosemite that had not been photographed before, but he now also took more extreme measures to get the pictures he wanted. As one contemporary writer described it:

114. The Flying Studio.

'The Flying Studio': the photographer's equipment in the field, one half of a stereograph, 1867.

'Yosemite Studies', 1872, one half of a stereograph in the *Valley of the Yosemite* series.

[Muybridge] has waited several days in a neighborhood to get the proper conditions of atmosphere for some of his views, has cut down trees by the score that interfered with the cameras from the best point of sight; he had himself lowered by ropes down precipices to establish his instruments where the full beauty of the object to be photographed could be transferred to the negative, has gone to points where his packers refused to follow him and has carried his apparatus himself rather than forego the picture on which he had set his mind.[12]

Muybridge's desire for the perfect picture made him oblivious to any danger. He climbed to the top of Yosemite Falls, rappelled down through the boulders, hung over the edge of high cliffs to photograph the chasms below and ventured out on a precipice to photograph across the Valley. In one picture he sits precariously on a rock overlooking the void, contemplating the emptiness around him (see page 96). Such risk-taking, and this photograph in particular, would be used later as evidence of his insanity.

He began by photographing along the Merced River on the Valley floor before moving up to the higher lands and cliffs from which he photographed the Sierra Nevada Mountains and, at the end of his trip, the Mariposa Grove. The resulting pictures, 'a series of eight hundred of the most perfect photographs ever offered for public inspection – some of them gems of art',[13] included stereos, full plate and mammoths. The mammoth plates in particular show an artist at the height of his powers and a photographer incorporating the lessons of the American landscape painters who had codified a myth of national identity through their depiction of the sublime.

Muybridge's photographs depict a paradisaical wilderness of rocks, precipices, mountains and water whose stark untrammelled beauty symbolized the freedom and regeneration that was at the core of the American experience of the 'new' West. There are few traces of humanity in this vision of virgin nature. Whereas his photographs of San Francisco have a picturesque quality that conveys social containment, Muybridge's Yosemite images project the viewer into an unbounded nature and describe the geological forces that shaped it. Many of his compositions even eliminate any sense of solid ground that might enable the viewer to find his or her footing in this vast emptiness, while emphasizing the precarious position of the photographer and drawing attention to the risks he takes.

Muybridge seated at the foot of 'Ulysses S. Grant', 1872, albumen print by an unknown photographer.

With their controlled tonal range, the pictures focus on dramatic contrasts of stasis and movement. As in 1867, Muybridge was fascinated by the intensity of the experience of rushing water in Yosemite, and he made many pictures of the falls and rivulets that tumbled over the ancient rocks. But the long exposure times required by the wet-plate process on the mammoth negatives rendered the falls as long horizontal ribbons of pale inchoate cloud. In pictures describing the effects of light and reflections on placid bodies of water such as Mirror Lake and the Merced River, he presents a more serene natural order of a transcendent nature. In both rushing and reflecting water, he emphasizes atmosphere and weather, combining images of billowing clouds and brilliant contrasts of light and shadow.

Muybridge also made photographs of the ancient glacier channel at Lake Tenaya and other glacier indications 'at the suggestion of Clarence King', the geologist and catastrophist whose six-year survey of the forty-ninth parallel numbered photographer Timothy O'Sullivan among its employees. For one of these pictures, which provides yet another example of the lengths to which Muybridge would go to achieve the best picture, he moved an unwanted boulder out of the way.

As he was leaving the Valley in November, Muybridge photo-graphed the grove of mammoth sequoia trees at Mariposa. And there he was photographed, seated on a box of plates marked 'Thomas Houseworth & Co.' at the base of the tree named after General Grant, a giant with a 67-foot (20.4-m) circumference and a height of 268 feet (81.7 m). Muybridge looks tired and bedraggled; his rough clothes and slumping posture betray the hard work of the previous months. The box upon which he sits suggests that Houseworth had given Muybridge supplies in return for photographs; the subsequent animosity that arose over Muybridge's photographs between Houseworth and the rival and even more successful publishers Bradley & Rulofson supports that premise. But the identity of the person who took the photograph remains a mystery. The most probable candidate is Houseworth employee Robert Fiske, but there were eight other photographers making pictures in Yosemite in 1872 and Muybridge could have sat for any one of them.[14]

Also at Mariposa, Muybridge photographed Albert Bierstadt painting the local Native Americans. Bierstadt, whose brother Charles was a photographer and whose visit to Yosemite in 1863 had been inspired by Watkins's 1861 photographs, was the most eminent of the American landscape painters of the sublime. Both Crocker and Stanford collected his work, and each time he visited San Francisco it was noted in the press. Bierstadt had been elected the first honorary member of the San Francisco Art Association in August 1871, and on 17 January 1872 he met Muybridge at the Association's annual reception, where Muybridge was the only member to exhibit photographs, 'some very effective views in Russian River Valley, the scenes selected with so much taste as to give them an artistic value'.[15]

Bierstadt had been in Yosemite since the early spring. When the two met, the painter asked Muybridge to make photographs of the Paiute that he could use for his sketches. In photographing the wonders of Yosemite, Muybridge had essentially ignored the Native Americans living there – and all other humans for that matter – in order to create a vision of sublime wilderness; but now, in the pictures he made at the Mariposa encampment, he rendered the Paiute vividly. His depiction is a kind of reportage on a way of life that was quickly disappearing. Once again the stereos form a sequence from far to near, beginning with the encampment photographed from the far bank of the Merced. A closer view of the camp is followed by a shot of the Paiute chief's lodge, not much more than a fragile construction of branches and planks, then a photograph of a ceremonial meeting of the 'Talkers', the people who recounted the tribe's traditions, since there was no written language. (Muybridge titled this last one *A Morning Concert on the Merced*.) The sequence continues with a family posed in front of their branch-and-leaf dwelling followed by a group of men in Western clothing seated on a log (titled '*Piute* [*sic*] *Bucks on a log*'); young men cooling off in the river ('*A Summer Day's Sport*'); an old woman and young boy in front of their hut; a '*Medicine Man Sleeping*'; a picture of a woman making bread; a portrait of five women ('*Mariposa Belles*'), arranged in a pyramidal composition and clothed in Western dress, who gaze at the camera; and a

'Albert Bierstadt's Studio', 1872, one half of a stereograph in *The Indians of California* series.

picture of the camp's sweat lodge. Muybridge's photograph of Bierstadt (*'Bierstadt's Studio'*) shows the painter in front of his easel sketching the 'Talkers' while one of the Paiute on the log glares at the camera. Bierstadt made more than one picture from this encounter. His 1872 painting *Mariposa Indian Encampment, Yosemite Valley, California* borrowed the lodges and figures from Muybridge's photographs; he painted the individual lodges twice, and in *'Indians in Council'*, showed the group of 'Talkers'. Bierstadt in turn influenced the photographer. Muybridge's small 'Yosemite Studies' featuring meandering streams and picturesque reflections were no doubt made with Bierstadt's encouragement for the use of artists.

Muybridge had left Flora alone for the entire summer and fall. But he spent the winter with her in the city, continuing to solicit subscriptions for and printing the Yosemite pictures. When he finally published them, in May 1873, he did so not from Nahl's but from Bradley & Rulofson's, now the most eminent gallery in the city and the only one to boast an elevator. They had promised Muybridge 'the finest production and distribution arrangement they could put together'[16] and the publication of a catalogue devoted to his work. Their aggressive marketing would increase Muybridge's prestige and give his photographs wider visibility.

Bradley & Rulofson issued a catalogue of Muybridge's *Yosemite* views complete with a backlist of most of his *Pacific Coast* scenes. The anonymously written catalogue introduction claimed that Muybridge was 'unrivalled in America' for his 'judicious selection of subject, artistic treatment, and skilful manipulation'. The value of Muybridge's subscription list, 'exceeding twenty thousand dollars, including one thousand dollars each from the Central and Union Pacific Railroad Companies, and five hundred dollars from the Pacific Mail Steamship company' was, according to the writer, 'something unprecedented in the history of Photographic publication'.[17]

An 1873 trade card for Bradley & Rulofson's Gallery of Photographic Art.

The measure of the marketability Muybridge's landscape photography attained can be taken by an incident that took place after his move to Bradley & Rulofson. Thomas Houseworth, the owner of the gallery that bore his name, believed he would be the one to publish Muybridge's Yosemite photographs. Three of the views had already appeared on Houseworth mounts. His disappointment at what he perceived to be a betrayal on Muybridge's part provoked an act of revenge. In the centre of his display window, Houseworth posted a dirty, crumpled Muybridge print on a Bradley & Rulofson mount. The response was swift. On 26 November 1873 a notice appeared in the *Bulletin*: 'Messrs Bradley and Rulofson are much obliged to Mr Houseworth for giving their names a place in his window; but attaching them to an old, soiled print from a condemned negative of Muybridge's (neither print nor negative being made by them) shows to what a wretched straight the poor gentleman is driven in a fruitless effort to compete in business'.[18]

Muybridge evidently took pleasure in the battle but set himself above the fray of competing commercial interests by taking out his own notice in the *Bulletin* three days later. He was, he said, like the lion irritated by an impudent ass in Aesop's fable, who 'conscious of his own power and the estimation placed upon his abilities silently pursued his own way, being too much occupied with his own business to allow his honoring so contemptible a detractor with the slightest notice'.

On 1 December Bradley & Rulofson again ran their attack ad, but this time Houseworth printed a rejoinder:

> The Yosemite view exhibited by us in our window is one of a set of forty furnished to a subscriber by Bradley and Rulofson for the sum of $100 and bears their name as the publishers. The View is a fair sample of the lot which was sold to me at a heavy discount on the cost and is now in the same condition as when received by the original purchaser. We would further remark that we had tried to purchase from these gentlemen some of their views and that they positively refused to sell us, for reasons which we leave others to judge.

The free publicity did nothing to damage Muybridge's reputation. The newspapers were full of praise both for the dramatic mammoth pictures and for the smaller 'views' that were similar in elegiac tone to his studies of clouds and trees. For all intents and purposes, Muybridge was now victorious over his rival Watkins. He was now fully Muybridge; and his fame as an artist was assured.

His renown as a documentary photographer was greatly enhanced that year too, when his photographs of the Modoc War, one of the last of the Indian conflicts, were published in *Harper's Weekly*. The traditional hunting grounds of the Modoc straddled the California and Oregon borders, as did those of their neighbours, the Klamath and Snake tribes. When the u.s. government decided to make their lands available for white settlers, the Modocs were herded onto a reservation in an area that included most of the Klamath lands, creating an intolerable situation. Led by the Modoc brave Kintpuash, who was known as 'Captain Jack', the Modocs twice defied the government by returning to their own lands on Lost River, just north of Tule Lake. In November 1872 the government tried to push them back. They resisted. Outnumbered two to one, for half a day the Modocs held off the Army, and then, after massacring settlers on the far shore in retaliation for the death of one of their warriors, they retreated to the Lava Beds, a lunar

The Modoc War. 'Mrs Riddell, (Toby, the Squaw who cautioned General Canby of his impending fate), and Riddell her husband', 1873, one half of a stereograph in *The Modoc War* series.

landscape of hills, caves and tunnels that became their stronghold for the next seven months.

The u.s. Army was now determined to wipe them out. On 17 January 1873, in dense fog, over 300 soldiers and volunteers from California and Oregon mounted an attack on some 50 to 75 Modocs, which resulted in the wounding or death of 37 soldiers. They had not actually sighted a single Modoc. The whites had no understanding of the difficult, barren terrain, which was dotted with shards of rock and broken with chasms and gulleys. The Modocs, on the other hand, knew it intimately; a nearby grazing herd and stolen food kept them going.

In February the government attempted a peace commission, sending an Indian woman, Matilda, and her white husband, Bob Whittle, to the Modoc stronghold together with Artina Choakus, also known as One-Eyed Dixie, a Modoc. For their part, the Modocs agreed to talk with Yreka resident Frank Riddle and his Modoc wife, Toby. Two unproductive meetings ensued in February and March. On 11 April the Modocs requested a third. Toby Riddle warned General Canby and the peace commissioners that the Indians were armed and dangerous, but her words went unheeded. The peace commissioners – General Canby, Revd Eleazer Thomas and Alfred Meacham, its chair – went to the peace tent accompanied by two Modocs, Bogus Charley and Boston Charley, where Jack repeated his demand that the Modoc land be returned, and then the meeting exploded. Jack shot Canby dead; Boston Charley shot Thomas dead. Meacham was wounded and the two other peace commissioners ran for their lives. That was on Good Friday. The following Tuesday, the war resumed in earnest. Nearly one hundred Indian scouts from central Oregon were summoned to bolster the more than 300 troops.

The newspaper reporters who had followed the war until this point had created sympathy across America, particularly in the East, for the plight of the Modocs. When word spread of the slaughter that had aborted the peace meeting, this sympathy largely evaporated. The death of the highly respected Canby, the only General ever to be killed in California's and Oregon's Indian wars, brought latent feelings of revenge to the surface.

The Modocs now had little to lose. They had been indicted for murder in Oregon and if captured would hang. The War Department named Jefferson C. Davis to replace Canby. Davis arrived in early May and reorganized the demoralized troops. He ordered them into the Lava Beds to track the Indians and, using Modoc tactics, to engage in skirmishes which resulted in many Modoc deaths.

In the end, however, it was dissent among the Modocs that put a stop to the war. Bogus Charley, Black Jim and Hooker Jim surrendered to Davis and promised to deliver Jack in exchange for their own lives. On 31 May fourteen other Modocs and their families 'quietly gave themselves up to the troopers'.[19] On 4 June, Jack surrendered, accompanied by one or two men, two boys, three women and some small children. He had held off the u.s. Army for all this time with only 70 men. He was hanged with Schonchin John and two others on 3 October at Fort Klamath. The other Modocs were exiled to Indian Territory in present-day Oklahoma. Without being informed of their destination, they were herded into boxcars on the new transcontinental railroad for the first and undoubtedly last trip they would ever take.

Muybridge arrived at the Army's main camp at the end of April (a few weeks after the *Alta California* had described his first experiments photographing Occident), in time to witness the final phase of the Modoc standoff. He accompanied chief army engineer Captain G. J. Lydecker, for whom he provided topographical images of the Lava Beds to help the War Department in Washington understand the difficulty of the terrain. On his own, Muybridge photographed the camps, the soldiers and the characters in the unfolding drama. His reputation for intrepid travel into inhospitable territory played no small role, and he wasn't intimidated by the Modocs. Indians had long figured in his photographs, at home

'A Modoc Brave on the War Path', 1873, one half of a stereograph in *The Modoc War* series.

in their own lands. What he was not able to photograph, however, was the conflict itself. The wet-plate exposure times were not fast enough to capture movement (although they would become so within a few years, thanks to Muybridge). Instead, as Roger Fenton had, in his pictures of the Crimean War in 1855, Muybridge focused on the setting and the players: the hiding places of the Modoc, the camps, the soldiers and generals, including Davis, and the Indian scouts who worked with them. And although the Modocs were as invisible to Muybridge as they were to the soldiers, he did try to show his audience the enemy by having a Warm Springs Indian scout pose with a rifle and titling the picture 'Modoc Brave Lying in Wait for a Shot', later published by Bradley & Rulofson as 'A Modoc Brave on the War Path'.

Muybridge's pictures became the primary visual record of the war. The conflict was heavily covered by the newspapers, with reporters swaying opinion first for, and then against, the Modocs' insistence on keeping their homelands. Engravings made from Muybridge's photographs were used to illustrate press accounts. Five of them, including *Toby, the Squaw who cautioned General Canby*, were published in *Harper's Weekly* on 21 June. And fifteen were published in 1914 in *The Indian History of the Modoc War* by Jefferson C. Riddle, the son of Toby and Frank.

A month later, in June, Muybridge headed north into Oregon to photograph the Columbia River and Cascade Mountains as well as a panorama in seven parts of Portland for his Bradley & Rulofson series *Pacific Northwest Scenes*. In late summer he photographed San Quentin prison. By September he received two pieces of important news: he had won the Gold Medal for his Yosemite pictures at the Vienna International Exhibition (a new World's Fair in Austria), and Flora was pregnant.

4

Love, Loss and Central America

Flora had been pregnant twice before, but both pregnancies had ended in stillbirths. This baby would live, but his birth led to a dramatic confrontation that threatened to destroy the successful life and reputation Muybridge had established in America.

Muybridge was away for much of this pregnancy leaving Flora in the care of a midwife, Susan Smith. At 2 am on 15 April 1874, Smith was woken by a loud knock on the door. Then, as Smith told it:

A tall gentleman in a white hat said that Mrs Muybridge wanted me immediately. I said that I would dress as soon as possible and go, but he cried out that she was in the carriage. I said that she must be brought into the house as I knew her condition but he said no, and half lifted me across the sidewalk. Mrs Muybridge was lying in the carriage (which had, as I learned afterward, just come from the Cliff House) and suffering the first stages of labor. We drove rapidly, I half clothed, to her residence, on the corner of Howard and Third. The child, a boy, was born at 4 o'clock on the following afternoon. Mr Muybridge at the time was out of town. I telegraphed for him and he came home the next day. He stayed for a week or ten days, until all danger was past and then he went away again. He went to Belmont on business. The day after he left, Mrs Muybridge wrote a note and told me to take it to the office of the *Evening*

Post and inquire for Major Larkyns . . . He called frequently, and while he was there I was always sent from the room.[1]

Major Harry Larkyns, like Muybridge, had come to San Francisco to remake himself. A charming adventurer, Larkyns was over six feet tall, robust and handsome in a roguish way. He claimed to have come from an illustrious background (related to the British royal family and heir to an Indian rajah) and to have led a life of unbelievable feats (fighting with Mazzini and Garibaldi in Italy and with the French in the Franco-Prussian War, at which time he supposedly was made a major and received the Legion of Honour).

Larkyns arrived in San Francisco in November 1872 along with a man named Arthur Neil. The two had met in Salt Lake City. Larkyns claimed that he was on his way to Japan and by some mistake his money and all his goods had been forwarded there by his express company. He asked Neil to advance him money until they arrived in San Francisco, where a bank credit of a thousand pounds sent by his grandmother was waiting for him. The two men lodged at the Occidental Hotel, which Neil paid for; he also paid the phenomenal bills for the wine and food they consumed, for Larkyns's entertainment of a certain 'notorious' young lady named Fanny and for a trip they took to Honolulu.

Eventually fed up, in March 1873 Neil lodged a complaint against Larkyns for obtaining money under false pretences. Larkyns was imprisoned the same day. On 16 March the *Chronicle* admonished, 'Let his fate serve as a warning to such young gentlemen amongst us who may be living on the credit of expected remittances.' He was put on trial the next morning, but Neil, succumbing once more to Larkyns' charm, dropped the charges.

Muybridge must have met Larkyns around this time. Flora seems already to have known him. According to Muybridge:

In the early part of 1873 [Larkyns] came into the gallery when I was at work. Mr Rulofson and Max Burkhardt, who were employed in the gallery, had known him for some time previous to this. He wanted to get some of my views for some purpose he had in mind, I do not now remember what. My wife, who sometimes worked in the gallery a little, touching up pictures, was present, and she introduced him to me. I had frequently heard her speak of Major Larkyns before, but did not know that she was much acquainted with him – but it seems they were better acquainted than I expected they were.

'After his introduction to me', Muybridge continued, 'he frequently came up to the gallery and I often gave him points in regard to art matters, which he was then writing about for the *Post*'. Larkyns worked for the *Post* as a drama critic and was supplied with tickets to the theatre; he often took Flora as his guest. For Flora, the charming Larkyns seemed the perfect gentleman, someone who enlivened her otherwise rather dreary existence with an older, often absent husband. At first, Muybridge saw no harm in allowing them to see each other. Though much more plentiful than before the war, single women of good social standing were still scarce in San Francisco, and it was not uncommon for married women to move in society in the company of single men. Muybridge wanted Flora to enjoy herself, and as the theatre held 'no attraction for him', he allowed her to go with Larkyns.[2] He was apparently oblivious, however, both to Larkyns's dodgy character and to the lonely Flora's need for more than a harmless flirtation.

In a later very public disclosure about the private matters of his marriage, Muybridge sounded bewildered:

We never had any trouble to speak of, we sometimes had little disputes about money matters but they were not serious. I was always a man of very simple tastes and few wants, and I did not spend much money. What I had left over after paying my little expenses I gave to her, and yet she was always wanting more. I could never see that she bought anything with it to speak of, or imagine what she did with it. We sometimes had little spats about the money but nothing serious – nothing more than married people have every day and forget the next.

Flora, of course, was spending money on Larkyns, whose tastes were extravagant. Muybridge was slow to suspicion, but when Flora stayed out all night on one occasion, Muybridge warned Larkyns the following morning: 'You know my right in the premises as a married man. So do I, and I shall defend them. If you transgress them again after this morning I shall hold you to the consequences and I suppose you know what that means in California.'[3]

Muybridge named the son who was born into such dramatic circumstances Floredo Helios, a fanciful combination of his wife's name and his pseudonym; but his joy in the child's arrival was dampened by his own mother Susannah's death three days later. Muybridge had not seen her for almost ten years, although they had continued to write to each other. In her will she left him and his brother Thomas, now a dentist in Walla Walla, Washington, fifty pounds each. Flora meanwhile recovered quickly from the birth and continued to see Larkyns whenever Muybridge left the house, which was often. The success of his Yosemite photographs prompted other commissions. Immediately after Floredo's birth, Muybridge was off to Belmont, eighteen miles (29 km) south of the city, to photograph the estate of W. C. Ralston. In May he made daily trips across the Bay to photograph the new University of California at Berkeley. In early summer he began a trip north to photograph the coast, but before leaving, perhaps aware at some level of Flora's increasing intimacy with Larkyns, he despatched her and Floredo to her uncle's family in The Dalles, Oregon. Totally absorbed once again with his work, he rarely wrote to Flora, who complained to friends that he didn't answer her letters.

If Flora had been a little wiser with her money, or a little less besotted with Larkyns, the tragedy that was about to unfold might have been avoided. Muybridge had given Flora a hundred dollars to pay the midwife Susan Smith and Flora had spent the money on herself and Larkyns. In the fall, after repeatedly being rebuffed by Muybridge in her requests for payment, Smith took him to court for the outstanding bill. To prove that it had never been paid, she showed Muybridge a letter written by Flora. The letter not only confirmed the unpaid bill, but also revealed the depth of Flora's passion for Larkyns. And Smith had two other letters: she had first acted as the go-between for the lovers but had stopped passing on their letters when her bill wasn't paid. At the hearing – the court ultimately ruled against Muybridge and ordered him to pay Smith $107 – Smith had given the letters to Muybridge's lawyer, a Mr Sawyer. Afterwards, Sawyer took Muybridge into his office where he showed him the letters. 'As I closed the door', Smith said, 'I heard a scream and a fall.'

On Saturday, 17 October, Muybridge came to Smith's house, looking 'more terrible than I had ever seen him. He appeared as though he had no sleep the night before.' In Smith's account:

He said: 'Mrs Smith are you busy? I want to see you.'

I told him I was not. I asked him in; he picked up a picture on the table and said with a start, 'Who is this?'

I said, 'It is your baby.'

He said: 'I have never seen this picture before. Where did you get it, and where was it taken.'

I said, 'Your wife sent it to me from Oregon. It was taken at Rulofson's.'

He turned over the picture and started, turning red and pale, and said: 'My God! What is this on the back of this picture in my wife's handwriting – 'Little Harry!' He stamped on the floor and exhibited the wildest excitement. His appearance was that of a madman; he was haggard and pale, his eyes glassy; his lower jaw hung down; [he] showed his teeth; he trembled from head to foot, and gasped for breath. He was terrible to look at.

He cried out: 'Great God! Tell me all!' He came forward with his hand upraised.

I said, 'I will tell you all', I thought he was insane, and would kill me or himself if I did not. I then told him all I knew.[4]

Smith's description of Flora's betrayal shattered Muybridge. He rushed to Rulofson's where, as the dealer later testified, 'He threw himself on a lounge and wept bitterly, moaning like a man in great distress of mind.' When he finally became sufficiently calm, he said,

Mr Rulofson, you have been a good friend to me. I want you to promise me that in the case of my death you will uphold the good name of my wife, and that you will settle our business affairs with her as you would with me.

Muybridge then told the whole story to Rulofson, vowing to go to Calistoga that day to hunt down Larkyns. 'One or the other of them must die', Muybridge said, and Rulofson could not hold him back.[5]

Muybridge took the train to Calistoga and then rented a carriage and driver to take him to the Yellow Jacket Mine, a part of the silver district north of the city where Larkyns was working as a surveyor and a correspondent for the *Stock Reporter*. According to the testimony of the driver, George Wolfe, Muybridge was calm, his conversation natural and rational. He arrived at the house of William Stuart, the mine's owner, was invited in and asked for Larkyns. 'I will only detain him a moment', Muybridge said. When

Larkyns called from the well-lit parlour where he was playing cards to the doorway where Muybridge stood, he couldn't see him clearly. 'Who are you?' Larkyns asked. 'My name is Muybridge and I have a message for you from my wife', Muybridge responded as he shot Larkyns at close range. The bullet pierced his chest. He collapsed as he tried to run back into the house. Muybridge stood stock-still. One of the card players disarmed Muybridge, who did not resist. Coolly, he apologized to the company for 'the interruption'. Larkyns was dead.[6]

In the custody of the driver and two other men, Muybridge was taken to Calistoga, where he was arrested and put into the Napa County Jail. Larkyns's body was returned to San Francisco, where his funeral attracted a large crowd, including 'a well-known actress for the California Theater who at the funeral leaned from her seat and, sobbing violently, put a handsome bouquet upon the coffin and, following it to the grave, was the last person to leave the vault'.[7]

Muybridge languished in the Napa jail for almost four months, charged with first-degree murder, a crime punishable by death. His trial began on 3 February and was over two days later. Because of his fame and the mixture of passion and violence that was the crux of his actions, the trial was attended by crowds of friends and curious onlookers and covered by reporters from all the newspapers. Their reports of the testimony give us the fullest description we have of Muybridge's character, personality and habits. Muybridge never expressed regret over what he had done. And why would he? He saw himself as a man betrayed by his wife, and he saw his wife as an innocent, led astray by a disreputable bounder. His was an act of retribution carried out by a man of passion, a romantic and an artist. And the jury would agree.

Muybridge's defence team, which consisted of three excellent lawyers led by William Wirt Pendegast, a friend of Stanford's and a former congressman, entered a plea of insanity. His witnesses attested to Muybridge's eccentricity. According to Silas Selleck, whom Muybridge had followed to San Francisco from New York, Muybridge was a different man after his stagecoach accident and subsequent disappearance:

> When he came back [to San Francisco] . . . he had changed so entirely that when he stood in my store, on his return, I could hardly recognize him – hardly know him. In some respects [I] do not consider him of sound mind; his brain is affected.

One Mr Gray, a music vendor who also knew Muybridge before his accident and after his return to San Francisco, noted that there was a 'marked change in him . . . He was formerly pleasant and agreeable; afterward, irritable, more careless in dress and not so good a businessman. He was untidy and his hair turned gray'. Rulofson claimed that Muybridge was quite mad. He was first and foremost unbusinesslike; he 'would never take a view for money if he did not see beauty in it but would drop his tools and pack up at once'. It was Rulofson who described Muybridge's activities in Yosemite, pointing to the picture where he is sitting on the edge of the rock with his feet dangling over a three-thousand-foot void. Worse still, he would 'stay up all night reading – generally some classical work'. Muybridge sounds like an exemplar of the romantic artist, but to these men such behaviour clearly indicated the actions of an insane man. Muybridge remained calm throughout the testimony and on 5 February took the stand. He recounted his stagecoach accident and how his good health was always afterward marred by headaches. Mrs Smith reported that he once said to her, '"I feel bad here sometimes", tapping his forehead'.

Even though the eyewitness testimony demonstrated that the crime was premeditated and in cold blood, after deliberating all night, the jury, all married men, returned a verdict of not guilty. Nor did they find Muybridge insane. Pendegast, a man with a

'Contemplation Rock, Glacier Point', 1872, one half of a stereograph in the *Valley of the Yosemite* series. The seated figure is Muybridge.

reputation for flowery oration, had closed his defence with the melodramatic plea

> to send [Muybridge] forth free – let him take up the thread of his broken life, and resume that profession upon which his genius has shed so much luster – the profession which is now his only love. Let him go forth into the green fields, by the bright waters, through the beautiful vallies, and up and down the swelling coast, and in the active work of securing shadows of their beauty by the magic of his art, he may gain 'surcease of sorrow' and pass on to his allotted end in comparative peace.[8]

This emotional speech was greeted with a round of applause.

Muybridge's response to the verdict was dramatic:

> A convulsive gasp escaped the prisoner's lips, and he sank forward from his chair. The mental and nervous tension that had sustained him for days of uncertain fate was removed in an instant and he became as helpless as a newborn babe. Mr Pendegast caught him in his arms and thus prevented his falling to the floor but his body was as limp as a wet cloth. His emotion became convulsive and frightful. His eyes were glassy, his jaws set, and his face livid. The veins of his hands and forehead swelled out like whipcord. He moaned and wept convulsively, but uttered no word of pain or rejoicing.[9]

According to another account,

> His face was absolutely horrifying in its contortions as convulsion followed convulsion. The Judge discharged the jury and hastily left the court room, unable to bear the sight . . . The clerk hid his face in his handkerchief . . . some of the jurors turned away to avoid the spectacle. Others gathered around to calm the prisoner, and all of them were moved to tears.

A doctor was sent for but it was one of Muybridge's lawyers, Johnston, who was able to pacify his client:

> [He] finally said sternly: 'Muybridge. I sympathize with you, but this exhibition of emotion is extremely painful to me, and for my sake alone I wish you to desist.' Muybridge suddenly straightened his form and said: 'I will, sir; I will be calm I am calm now.' And then his emotion subsided, so that in a quarter of an hour he was able to go upon the street.

The judge returned, and Muybridge was formally discharged from custody and left the courtroom. Outside he was greeted by a raucous welcoming crowd, and the reporter noted that

> The jury discarded entirely the theory of insanity . . . acquitted the defendant on the ground that he was justified in killing Larkyns for seducing his wife. This was directly contrary to the charge of the Judge, but the jury do not mince the matter or attempt to excuse the verdict. They say that if their verdict was not in accord with the law of the books, it is with the law of human nature; that, in short, under similar circumstances they would have done as Muybridge did, and they could not conscientiously punish him for doing what they would have done themselves. This fact was recognized fully and freely, by Judge, jury and counsel and prisoner. The latter still denies the correctness of the insanity theory as he did before the trial, saying that he knew what he was doing when he sought Larkyns and killed him, and he did it designedly. Muybridge came down to this city in the evening. He conversed freely with his friends on the way about the trial and his intended future movements. For his wife he uniformly, after his arrest, spoke in pity rather than passion. Since his acquittal he has spoken in the same spirit, saying that he should always regard her with compassion for her fallen estate, and that so long as he lives and has a dollar or the means of getting one she shall not come to want.[10]

Flora had returned to San Francisco with Floredo sometime after the murder, a penniless outcast. On 14 December 1874, while Muybridge awaited trial, she had made the first application for divorce on grounds of extreme cruelty and asked for alimony. Her suit reveals just how successful Muybridge had become. Flora claimed her husband had personal property and money valued at between five and ten thousand dollars (the equivalent of about $50,000 to $100,000 today) and that he earned more than $600 a month.

The application for divorce was denied. Shortly after the trial, Flora attempted to seize Muybridge's cameras when he left town for South America: 'While the relentless wife was taking steps to lay an embargo, her estranged husband vanished in the mists hovering over the bar.'[11] On 27 March 1875 her suit was denied a second time. When she went to court again at the beginning of April, however, having read the press descriptions of his temper and eccentricity, she made her allegations of cruelty more concrete. She said that Muybridge had falsely charged her with the crime of adultery, and 'threatened to kill her . . . [and that] from that time until she left for Oregon, she lived with him in fear of her life. So anxious was she to go to Oregon that she went to the boat on foot, carrying her infant, when she was scarcely able to walk. Her fears were increased by her knowledge that Muybridge's character was fitful, violent and jealous.' She claimed too that Muybridge had paid for her divorce from her first husband, but also that he abused her, demanding back money he had given her to buy clothes when she didn't spend it, threatening 'that if she did not marry him he would be revenged upon her', and, most fanciful of all, given what we know of his character, she alleged 'the commission of adultery on Muybridge's part in the summer of 1874'.[12] This time the judge listened. Muybridge was directed to show cause why he shouldn't have to pay alimony during the pending of the divorce action, and on 30 April, noting that 'Muybridge was in the photographic business and would seem to be in the receipt of from $200 to $400 a month' and that he 'would appear to be both a leading and prosperous man in his profession',[13] the court ordered him to pay Flora $50 a month, backdated to January, until the divorce was granted. But it was too late. In July 1875 she died suddenly (and, to some, suspiciously) from 'a stroke of paralysis' according to the 19 July *Examiner* or 'complication of [a] spinal complaint' (19 July

Chronicle). Her last words were reputed to be 'I'm sorry', but to whom, and for what, she was apologizing is not clear. She was 24.

In a pathetic postscript, more than a year after Flora's death, her lawyer, one J. B. Hart, made a motion to be substituted as plaintiff in her divorce suit against Muybridge, 'to recover certain moneys advanced to Mrs Muybridge during her illness and poverty, and also to recover payment for services rendered her. Some jocose remarks were indulged in by counsel to the peculiar position Mr Hart would occupy if the motion were granted'.[14]

Muybridge moved Floredo to the Protestant Orphan Asylum in San Francisco and without ever acknowledging or denying the child's paternity continued to pay for his board. From the age of ten, Floredo worked as a ranch hand, seemingly more comfortable with horses than with people. He became an alcoholic and died in Sacramento, killed by a car in 1944.

Less than two weeks after he was set free, Muybridge saw to his affairs in San Francisco, packed his equipment and clothes and set sail for Central America. He had planned the trip before the Larkyns tragedy. The Pacific Mail Steamship Company had commissioned him to make a series in Panama and Guatemala in the hopes of enticing potential travellers to the region and potential investment in Guatemalan coffee plantations. The Pacific Mail had the monopoly on coffee export transportation and had once dominated the Panama to San Francisco route, until it lost most of its passenger business to the transcontinental railroad. The directors believed that photographs showing a peaceable, beautiful and progressive region might reverse their fortunes.[15]

Muybridge's arrival was noted by the *Panama Star* on 10 March 1875:

It is gratifying to know that he comes now to illustrate by view all the curious places that a traveller by Railroad and Pacific Mail Company's ships can see or be within reach of in a journey from

New York to San Francisco via this Isthmus. We have no doubt Mr Muybridge will find around Panama many views worthy of his peculiar photographic talent, and which will command a prominent place among the extra-tropical landscapes with which he has already enriched art galleries and expensive illustrated publications in the United States.

He took pictures for two months, making establishing shots of the area and then closing in on specific monuments and the people. He began with overviews of Panama City from the railroad bridge and the wharf, then after eight pictures made from the top of the city walls, he homed in on the churches, first those ruined in earth-quakes and then the large cathedrals and newer churches. He next took photographs of the cemetery, where he captured a burial as well. Moving to the commercial and government buildings, he photographed the palace of the president and the Pacific Mail Steamship office before focusing on people, subjects from 'old Panama' and finally the bay.

Muybridge's Panama is a study of contrasts – between the past, evoked by native traditions and ruined churches crumbling beneath vines and tree branches, and the present, epitomized by well-maintained city buildings and the ever-present colonizers. In *Native Hut* and two pictures called *Laundry*, the half-naked Mayan Indians are posed awkwardly before his cameras, while the white overseers in these same images scrutinize both the natives and the photographer. A series called *Native Women* presents the women frontally at middle distance. They stare balefully at the camera. In three pictures, they pose topless, wearing only their skirts; in one, the woman still holds in her hands the garment she has just taken off, presumably at Muybridge's behest. In another, Muybridge has tacked up a white sheet between two trees to set off the dark skin of a woman who stands facing the camera, holding a shallow basin on her head beside a seated child.

'Native Woman', 1875, one half of a stereograph in the *Isthmus of Panama* series.

From the bay, Muybridge travelled to Colón – it was then called Aspinwall, after William Henry Aspinwall, one of the Pacific Mail's founders and a promoter of the railroad across the Isthmus – to photograph the wharf, lighthouses and statues, and then to the Chagres region, where he made three pictures of its very primitive thatched-roof dwellings and the Mayan Indians who inhabited them. *The City Front* depicts a small boy in a shirt, wearing a hat that hides his face; in the background behind him, photographed on a diagonal, is a row of rickety huts. *The Principal Street* is even more tongue-in-cheek: the picture features a naked boy standing on a long piece of bark straddling a ditch.

Two months later, on the eve of Muybridge's departure for Guatemala, the *Star* again promoted the work:

> We can therefore congratulate all Central Americans that in Mr Muybridge they have an artist who will do for their interesting section of America what has never been so well done for it before, either by pen or pencil, in making it become known. We heartily recommend him to our friends and to all lovers of Art, official or private, in any part of Central America to which he may be able to carry his photographic apparatus, his talents, and his commendable social as well as artistic qualities.[16]

The comment on his social qualities suggests that Muybridge's immersion in this colonial society carved out of the jungle may have helped to ease his memory of the murder and the trial, offering emotional solace in the ruins and 'otherness' of the natives, although the photograph of the burial, unique in his oeuvre, might indicate a lingering melancholy.

From Panama, Muybridge sailed on the *Honduras* to El Salvador, stopping at La Unión to photograph its soldiers and from thence to San José, the port of Guatemala, and overland to Guatemala City, his base for the next five months. He arrived in a country undergoing a radical transformation, begun in 1871, when the Liberal Party defeated the pro-Mayan Indian Conservative government, heralding a shift away from a traditional rural economy of small landholdings (held both privately, by the Spanish colonizers or the mixed-blood *ladinos*, and communally by the predominantly indigenous population) toward a modern industrialized society.

The Guatemalan economy, traditionally dependent on the production and export of the red dye cochineal, had been destroyed

'Chagres. The Principal Street', 1875, one half of a stereograph in the *Isthmus of Panama* series.

by the German invention of synthetic dyes. The Liberal government under the reform-minded presidency of Justo Rufino Barrios responded by establishing a single new agribusiness – the growth, processing and exportation of coffee. Coffee production required considerable land, a large labour pool, capital investment in credit institutions (there were no banks in the country before 1874), expensive machinery and infrastructure: the roads, railroads and ports needed to export the product abroad. Under the Barrios goverment, all these requirements were met, but at great cost. By the 1880s the country's entire economy relied on the export of coffee. It had become a monoculture, dependent on foreign carriers such as the Pacific Mail and foreign markets and capital, in particular that of the United States.

Muybridge's task was to document the colonial architecture of the cities and the wonders of coffee growing in the countryside. His pictures of Guatemala City – especially the National Bank (opened in 1874), the University of Guatemala (secularized and made a state institution in 1875), the Carrera theatre, the city prison and the Sociedad Económica, built for the encouragement of agriculture, industry and the fine arts – all epitomize the success of liberal modernization. As a foreigner and emissary of the Pacific Mail, he was greeted everywhere. The many pictures of soldiers, military bands and politicians massed in the city squares of the coffee-producing towns of Quezaltenango and Mazatenango that he titled *Reception of the Artist* (he had made a picture of the same subject and with the same title in Panama), underlined not only his own importance, but also that of the company, under whose aegis he was travelling.

But Muybridge's artistic eye also captured the disappearing traditions of agrarian life in images of the carts and oxen that still transported goods; the cactus plantations with the last vestiges of the cochineal industry; the circular stone public laundries in the centre of towns; the fields in the mountains where the Mayan Indians still grew corn, beans and wheat; the local markets, usually surrounding the fountain that decorated the main plaza of the town; and the indigenous people themselves, the largest segment of the country's population, now slowly being reduced to serfdom on the consolidated tracts of land the government had taken from them and given over to private landowners for the cultivation of coffee.

Muybridge's 1875 photo-essay on coffee production described every phase in detail: clearing the land, planting seeds, transplanting young trees, picking the beans, spreading them to dry and husking and bagging them; he even followed the bags as they were carried by oxcart to the coast and photographed them being loaded onto boats. Muybridge had an entrée to all the plantations, but made most of his photographs at Las Nubes, the plantation of Pacific Steamship agent William Nelson. The photographs emphasize the hard labour that went into bringing the commodity to market. As Muybridge pictures them, the Mayan Indians who do the clearing and planting seem to blend into the landscape, small antlike creatures dotting the hills. He shows the pickers in groups squatting on the ground at dinnertime or the men and women celebrating together on a feast day. He photographs the women on their own, half-naked with large baskets of coffee beans on their heads, their lack of clothing signalling that they are 'primitives', as if they existed outside of history. Clothed, they stand on ladders to pick the berries and then bring them to the drying platforms, where the men wait to spread them. A picture of a group of women weaving and making cornmeal communicates the peaceful nature of the people as well as their self-sufficiency and independence – in other words, they are presented as good neighbours for Americans who might wish to invest in the country.

As he had done previously, Muybridge made many pictures from a bird's-eye view, here to establish the arrangement of the drying platforms and mills, before taking other images from close-up. The photographs of the modern mill equipment and the plantation owners in their European dress, standing on well-manicured lawns, suggest what is possible once the wilderness has been tamed.

At the beginning of October, the last month of his sojourn, Muybridge made another name change, but it was only temporary. As Sr D. Eduardo Santiago Muybridge ('Santiago' is a more lofty Spanish translation of 'James' than the more humble Jaime or Diego), he advertised, in Spanish, 'over two-hundred views'[17] for sale together with his Pacific Coast stereos. In November, back in

Panama, he again advertised his photographs of both that country and Guatemala. The *Star* reported that

> Those who take an interest in the fine arts and at the same time wish to obtain a series of views which will in fact constitute a pictorial history of Panama as seen in 1875, can see the specimen pictures, and order the number they desire, which will be sent from San Francisco, where they will be printed, under the superintendence of Mr Muybridge, which is itself a guarantee that they will be the finest specimens of the kind that can be produced by photography.[18]

On 27 November, Muybridge was home again in San Francisco, where he began the work of printing and mounting a selection of the more than 400 pictures he had made on his South American trip.

Muybridge had expected the Pacific Mail Steamship Company to pay his printing expenses and to buy a complete set of the pictures, but the company insisted that his free passage was the only bargain they had made. Muybridge once more sold his large pictures by subscription, offering portfolios of 120 prints for $100 gold. These and other formats were published from 618 and 620 Clay Street, the address of Henry W. Bradley, one half of Bradley & Rulofson. In his testimony at Muybridge's trial, Rulofson had gone into such detail when describing Muybridge's 'eccentricity' that the artist never forgave him and subsequently abandoned the company as his publisher, but stayed loyal to Bradley.

Muybridge printed his Central America photographs in different formats for different markets. Besides the single pictures for subscription sales, he printed a group as lantern slides that were projected at the Photographic Art Society meeting of 7 January 1876, although he was not present. A series on Panama alone was published in an 'Imperial' carte-de-visite format, and the photographs of Guatemala were used to illustrate 'A Trip to

Central America', an account in *Scribner's Monthly* of the travels of Ellsworth Westervelt, a New York merchant and an exemplar of a potential investor.[19]

Westervelt's description of his arrival in Guatemala City through the picturesque sugar mills, cochineal plantations and glistening lakes is thoroughly captured in Muybridge's pictures. They are at once documents of unfamiliar sites and artistic visions of dramatic scenes. The ruined churches brought down by earthquakes and gradually subsiding back into the jungle are rendered atmospheric, emphasizing the natural forces slowly strangling and eroding the crumbling stone, while the matter-of-fact portrayals of coffee cultivation express the promise of prosperity in the region.

Muybridge also published a selection of photographs in an album titled *The Pacific Coast of Central America and Mexico: The Isthmus of Panama; Guatemala; and the Cultivation and Shipment of Coffee. Illustrated by Muybridge, San Francisco, 1876.* The frontispiece consists of a photo collage, including a portrait of the 45-year-old Muybridge visibly aged, with his hair and beard almost completely white. Each of the remaining pictures in the album is captioned in his hand, clarifying the subject's locations and narrating the story of his travels and the story of coffee. He astutely made presentation copies of the album to give to Leland Stanford's secretary Frank Shay and to Jane Stanford, as well as to the widow of William Wirt Pendegast, who had died the previous February. On 25 May 1876, in reply to Mrs Pendegast's letter of thanks for his gift, Muybridge reveals some of the emotions he felt:

My dear Madam,
    Your kind note afforded me much happiness in its perusal, although I feel I am entirely undeserving of the thanks you so kindly proffer me.
    It is I who should and do thank you for permitting me to offer you so slight an acknowledgment of my lasting appreciation of

the noble and disinterested generosity shown me by your late husband when I bowed down by grief and crushed with broken pride so sadly needed the support and friendship I received from him. To my dying day I shall ever cherish his memory as that of the best and dearest friend I ever had.[20]

Muybridge also presented an album to a Mr Schrewin, president of the Pacific Mail Steamship Company, along with his bill. It was refused. Muybridge once again threatened a lawsuit, but because there was no contract to back up his claim, he didn't pursue it.

'Loading Carts for the Port at Las Nubes', 1875, one half of a stereograph in the *Central America* series.

Frontispiece to Muybridge's *The Pacific Coast of Central America and Mexico; the Isthmus of Panama; Guatemala; and the Cultivation and Shipment of Coffee*, 1876.

'Church of El Carmen, S. America destroyed by earthquake 1774', 1875, one half of a stereograph in the *Central America* series.

Muybridge's Central America tour was an artistic as well as financial success. The photographs won the Gold Medal at the Eleventh Industrial Exhibition in San Francisco, where the jury noted that

> For judicious selection of subjects, artistic taste and skilful manipulation, this artist has for many years stood at the head of his profession . . . These last productions of his camera

surpass all his previous efforts, and their examination renders it difficult to believe, that with our present knowledge and taste, photography can make much further progress toward absolute perfection.[21]

5

Panoramic San Francisco

In 1873 three of the 'Big Four', the investors who had created the Central Pacific Railroad, decided to move their head offices from Sacramento to San Francisco. With the company's move, Stanford, Crocker and Hopkins (Huntington had moved East as the company's New York agent) together with financial director David Colton began to amass land on which to build their houses on California Street Hill, a 300-foot (90-m) ridge that once marked the city's western boundary.

Thanks to the railroad, San Francisco was now the largest metropolis in the West, a centre of wealth and commerce distinguished not only by its saloons and dance halls but also by its new theatres, libraries and government buildings, whose construction Muybridge had followed with his cameras. Its inhabitants were no longer a shifting mass of immigrant labourers living in shanties, or transients seeking their fortune, but a stable and growing population of working, middle-class and wealthy families. The look of the city itself began to change as well. With a desire for aesthetic development, surveyors and city officials planned and laid out streets and plazas in an orderly fashion; and the sand hills that interrupted the city's expansion were either levelled or became the sites of homes for the elite.

California Street Hill was one such peak, considered to be the best real estate in the city. A refuge from the commercial centre and harbour, it commanded a view of the Bay from Berkeley to the Golden Gate. Mining, railroad and financial magnates began to build their mansions there in the late 1860s, when the area was nicknamed 'Nob Hill'. In 1873 Stanford, Hopkins and Crocker amassed land that surpassed all previous investments on the hill. Stanford bought an entire block in two purchases, and then divided it into two parts, selling half to Hopkins and keeping half for himself.

Their houses were intended to signal both their personal prosperity and the progress of civilization across the continent. Monstrously large and ornate, they became the most visible icons of the wealth and power of their owners, marrying social status to geographical prominence. As Robert Louis Stevenson later wrote, 'The great net of straight thoroughfares lying at right angles, east and west and north and south over the shoulders of Nob Hill, the hill of palaces, must certainly be counted the best part of San Francisco. It is there that the millionaires are gathered together vying with each other in display'.[1]

During the long economic depression that began in America that year, the directors' ostentatious houses were amongst the most visible manifestations of the enormous disparity between the thousands of jobless San Franciscans and the millionaires on the hill. 'These same thoroughfares that enjoy for a while so elegant a destiny have their lines prolonged into more unpleasant places. Some meet their fate in the sands; some must take a cruise in the ill-famed China quarters; some run into the sea; some perish unwept among pig-styes and rubbish-heaps.'[2] This extreme social stratification was brought to the boiling point in October 1877 when, under the leadership of Denis Kearney, an Irish-born teamster who galvanized the discontent of the unemployed, 3,000 men came to the hill to demonstrate their grievances against 'both the Chinese workers who had allegedly stolen their jobs and the railroad barons who had done so much to bring the Chinese to California'.[3] The result was not what they had hoped for, however: the state senate passed a law to increase the police force and to make incendiary speech illegal. Nob Hill and its residents were protected.

With its 41,000 square feet (3,810 square metres) divided into fifty rooms, Stanford's house was the largest private residence in California. Its size and its cost, said to be between one and two million dollars, made it grander even than anything New York City could boast.[4] It was intended as a centre of higher culture in the city, with music rooms, a library, a gallery, and rooms for receptions and balls. On 19 May 1875 Stanford described in the *Chronicle* his vision for the yet-to-be-completed palace:

> I shall hope to live to sit upon yonder balcony and look down upon a city embracing in itself and its suburbs a million of people . . . I shall see cars from the city of Mexico and trains laden with the gold and silver bullion and grain that comes from Sonora and Chihuahua on the south and from Washington Territory and Oregon on the north . . . I shall look out through the Golden Gate and I shall see fleets of ocean steamers bearing the trade of India, the commerce of Asia, the traffic of the islands of the ocean . . .

Three years earlier Muybridge had photographed Stanford's house in Sacramento. Now the former governor invited him to document his modern Xanadu after it was finished in early fall 1876.

Unlike the photographs he took in Sacramento, Muybridge's pictures of the Nob Hill mansion did not include any of its three inhabitants: Jane, Leland and their son Leland Junior. The first subjects of Muybridge's photographs were the lavish and grandiose interiors designed not by Jane Stanford but by the Pottier & Stymus Manufacturing Company of New York. Interior decoration was an entirely new field at this time, and the fact that Stanford hired professionals from the East reveals the importance he placed on achieving the right effect. The Stanford mansion was an emblem of its owner's wealth and business prowess – more like a royal palace, which is precisely how Muybridge photographed it.[5] He began with the Italianate exterior: its three stories of windows framed by pilasters and crowned with a pediment, the rusticated stone of the first storey and the large portico over the formal entry. He then photographed the rooms in a narrative of excess that moved from entrance to reception and library, and included sitting room, conservatory, dining room, picture gallery, salon, breakfast room and ballroom. The pictures incorporated the ceiling decorations in each room and from more than one point of view so that every object in every space could be catalogued.

Many of the photographs emphasize Stanford's connoisseurship: the 'Pompeian Room' peopled by the neoclassical sculptures he collected, decorated with mosaics and porcelain, and awash in swags of heavy drapery; the 'gentleman's library' that contained 3,000 volumes; the Chinese furniture given to him by the Chinese government at the Philadelphia Centennial for one of the bedrooms; and the 'Picture Gallery', whose damask-covered walls were hung with both European and American landscape paintings. Other photographs feature the mechanical conveniences that Stanford had installed, including an elevator and an 'electric orchestrion' in

Hall looking towards the Back Mosaic Floor, residence of Leland Stanford, San Francisco, 1877, albumen print.

the music and art room. Still others, as indicated by Jane Stanford's pencilled notations under the photographs, celebrate the colours of the fabrics and walls as well as particular pieces of furniture and objects in each room, documenting the latest in furnishings, textiles, woodwork and interior decoration.

By the late 1880s, the mansion would become even less of a family residence and more of a museum – the Stanfords continued to fill it with antiquities and treasures the family accumulated but they lived there only intermittently. After her husband's death in 1893, Jane Stanford began proceedings to transfer the house and its contents to Stanford University, which the couple had founded in 1891, but the transfer was never completed. On 19 April 1906 the uninhabited house, 'with all its treasure',[6] was destroyed in the fires that erupted following the great earthquake.

Muybridge's photographs, made 30 years earlier, survive in two duplicate albums. They are more than just the surviving records of a mythical mansion. In them, we see the perfect meeting of patron and artist. Using all his skills as a photographer and his expertise with lighting and composition, Muybridge undertook a portrait of the house that goes beyond mere topographical and architectural description. His images of the ghostly-lit cavernous rooms with their complex decorative schemes proclaim Stanford's taste, wealth, and public persona to the whole world.

When his assignment ended, Muybridge turned his camera to the city below. From three locations on the mansion's roof, he made seven images creating a visible record of the vision Stanford had described in the pages of the *Chronicle*. Placed in an album with the pictures of the house, the photographs form a discontinuous panorama that foretold the next project he would undertake – a panorama of the city from atop Nob Hill.[7]

Invented in 1787 by the English landscape painter Robert Barker, the painted panorama had by the mid-nineteenth century come to rival the stereograph as one of the most popular forms of mass entertainment. But whereas stereo cards were viewed and enjoyed in the privacy of the home, the panorama was a public entertainment and theatrical spectacle. The first panoramas were 360-degree paintings, the most popular subjects being famous cities and battles. To experience them, spectators had to climb a staircase into a rotunda especially made for their viewing. Surrounded by the picture at eye level, the viewer would move through both space and time while examining the vista.

The 1840s saw the rise in popularity – especially in the United States – of an even more ambitious entertainment, the moving panorama. Accompanied by a narrator, towering painted rolls of canvas were slowly unfurled, transferred from one gigantic spool to another by unseen stage hands hidden behind a proscenium, presenting a continuous, unfolding scene to a seated audience. The most popular of the American moving panoramas described current events such as the Mexican–American and Civil Wars and the expansion of the Western frontier. The three key themes to emerge in the latter category were travel along the Mississippi River, stories of overland exploration and migration, and the growth of San Francisco.[8] Like stereos, the narrated panoramas gave new meaning to the concept of armchair travel. These spectacles melded entertainment and education, combining emotion-laden narratives of American life and information about distant places and events.[9]

Daguerreotypes were sometimes used as sources for the painted panoramas because they were believed to enhance the accuracy and authenticity – and therefore the credibility – of what the paintings showed. On their own, photographic panoramas could not compete with their painted cousins. Being smaller, more personal and private, a photographic panorama forever froze a particular moment in time and space but did not convey a sense of duration and flow. Any movement in the photographs had to be bestowed by the viewer, whose eyes travelled over the pictures hung on a wall, spread out on a table or, with the stereo, placed in a viewer. Even then, the insistent physical borders of the photographs impeded any sense of a fluid continuum. Nonetheless, the popularity of panoramas made it inevitable that photographers would want to make them; as early as 1851, multiplate daguerreotype panoramas of Mississippi views and California scenes were being exhibited.

When it came to commercial appeal, photographic panoramas of San Francisco (and, on a smaller scale, other cities of the West), could actually compete with painted panoramas. The many hills of the city were perfect vantage points from which to photograph the buildings below and the Bay and islands beyond. The photographs could depict in more profuse detail (and more readily) the city's rapid growth, destruction and rebuilding – showing the construction of buildings and roads almost as it occurred. With the increasing use of the wet plate from the 1860s, photographic panoramas of San Francisco became an established genre. None was more spectacular, however, than the mammoth 360-degree view of the city that Muybridge would complete in 1878.

By then, Muybridge was adept at panoramas. In 1868 he had produced a seven-part stereo panorama of San Francisco from Rincon Point. In 1873 he had made a five-part panorama of the Army encampment partially surrounding Tule Lake during the Modoc War and in 1875 a beautiful eleven-part panorama of Guatemala City. In 1877 he completed his first 360-degree panorama of San Francisco, taken from the tower of the still unfinished Hopkins house next to Stanford's.

When Muybridge began in June, there were at least 50 panoramic views of San Francisco already in existence, though with very few exceptions, Carleton Watkins's 1870 twenty-stereo set *Panorama from Telegraphic Hill* among them, they were limited to 90- or 180-degree views.[10]

Muybridge's ambition was greater and presented formidable conceptual and technical difficulties. He had to transport all the glass and chemicals to make the wet-plate negatives to Hopkins's tower as well as his cameras and tripod. To capture the views, he had to position the camera, make an exposure and develop each negative immediately (he had at least one assistant for this). But then the real challenge began. He had to move the camera in such a way as to ensure that the horizon line was the same in each negative and that the edges of one image overlapped with the next. Aligning the horizon posed the greatest problem. Either the tripod had to be moved with exact precision or the camera had to be pivoted on the tripod. Because nineteenth-century tripods had no built-in levelling devices, any change in the ground meant that the horizon line in the pictures would be on different levels. Finally, he had to work fast enough so that the shifting shadows on the buildings as the sun moved through the sky would not be too noticeable.

Muybridge decided to divide the circumference of his subject into eleven parts and began to make his negatives – at least two from each vantage point – on a clear June morning. He started with a view to the southwest, pointing at Lone Mountain, and then moved his camera eleven times in a clockwise direction away from the sun. When he ended, about five hours later, the sun had moved 90 degrees, as can be seen by the change in the shadows cast by the buildings in the first and last pictures.[11]

Muybridge was not alone in photographing from the top of Nob Hill that June. Watkins was working next door on a six-part stereo panorama from the grounds of Stanford's mansion and then shortly thereafter, he began a second from the roof of Charles Crocker's, the large house that bookends Muybridge's panorama. Watkins 'had an unobstructed view of the entire city: to the north lay North Beach and Alcatraz and Angel islands; to the north-east, Telegraph Hill; to the east, the docks and the retail and commercial centre of the city; and to the south, Rincon Point and Mission Bay'.[12] But Muybridge had more.

He published his 1877 panorama in two formats. First, as eleven mounted albumen prints backed by a sheet of linen that was accordion-folded into an album and accompanied by a separate Key, and second, as a set of eleven 5 x 8¼-inch (12.7 x 21 cm) *boudoir* cards. Both the album and the cards were made from the same negatives, but Muybridge cropped, printed, mounted and presented the images differently. He felt free to assemble the panorama according to his aesthetic aims. For example, he did not publish the album prints in the order in which they were made: the tenth image was the first one taken that morning, while the one published as the ninth was in fact the last. Moreover, as David Harris has noted, Muybridge curiously integrated into the album format a print made from a negative belonging, by its cropping, to the *boudoir* set.[13]

The Key, which Muybridge copyrighted separately from the panorama, is his inventive promotional tool for this work. On this 8 x 12 inch (20.3 x 30.5 cm) card, he assembled the panorama's elements according to the dictates of publicity, rather than replicating the sightlines of a pivoting viewer. He divided the picture into three bands stacked on top of each other, each with its own distinct horizon line that defines it as a separate picture. The top shows the Bay from Golden Gate to the beginning of Telegraph Hill; the middle, divided again, is of downtown; and the bottom captures the length of the peninsula. Underneath the strip is a list of 221 buildings shown, keyed to corresponding numbers in the pictures above. Besides landscape features, offices, commercial buildings and churches, Muybridge also numbered each private residence. And not just the mansions of the rich, such as Stanford's and Crocker's, but smaller houses as well. The listing of the names of the owners of these more modest houses alongside the town's wealthiest citizens suggests that 'Muybridge was as much concerned with marketing his images to interested residents as he was with producing a definitive listing of the city's elite.'[14]

Right at the centre of the key, Muybridge placed a square to advertise his work: under the single dramatic name *Muybridge* is written 'Landscape, Marine, Architectural and Engineering'. Under the single word *Photographer* is stamped 'Official photographer of the u.s. Government and Grand Prize Medalist of the Vienna Exhibition, 1873'. Below that he lists the range of his work:

Reproductions of paintings drawings and Art Manufacture.
Photographic illustrations Of Alaska California Mexico Central
America and the Isthmus of Panama.
Horses photographed while running at full speed.

Finally he credits 'Copyright by Muybridge' and 'Morse's Gallery 417 Montgomery Street'.

The advertisement tells us where Muybridge was in August 1877. He had changed his galleries again and had made his mark as a copyist, exhibiting 21 photographic reproductions he had made of Norton Bush's paintings of Peru at the Art Association Galleries in February. In a fascinating footnote to his better-known exploits, Muybridge anticipated modern microfiche when he also proposed copying the public records of the town of San Jose, compressing them to a sixth of their original size both as a way of making them easier to store and as a method of avoiding the errors that occurred when they were hand-copied. But although the idea got plenty of coverage in the local *San Jose Mercury*, the city board thought it too expensive – at 35 cents a page – and imagined that the photographs would be too small to be readable.

As usual, Muybridge marketed his work through the newspapers. He announced his panorama – the 'only panorama of San Francisco ever published . . . nearly eight feet long . . . mounted in book form, or suitable for framing' – in the *Bulletin* on 11 July and in the *Alta* three days later. The response from critics was unanimously positive:

the work was singled out for praise in the *Chronicle* on 14 and 15 July and in the *Alta* on 22 July.

In September Muybridge published a prospectus from Morse's Gallery describing the remarkable clearness of the atmosphere on the day he took the photographs and emphasizing the clarity with which 'all the public buildings, hotels and banks, all the wharves, with very few exceptions and nearly all the stores and private residences within a radius of six miles [were] clearly distinguishable, the whole forming a complete Panorama of the entire city, its picturesque suburbs and surrounding ranges of hills'. Adding a description of the panorama's size and length, he offered it for sale postage-free, mounted for ten dollars gold, or unmounted and rolled up for eight.[15]

Muybridge also advertised on the verso of the *boudoir* cards, reproducing in letterpress the *Alta California*'s praise: The pictures 'make a complete circuit of the horizon', the reporter writes, showing 'that among the many wonderful features of our city, the panoramic character of its topography is not the least deserving of attention, though it has been overlooked, at least by people generally, until Muybridge discovered and utilized its artistic value'.[16] Muybridge printed in full the reporter's metaphor for the experience of viewing the panorama:

> Let us imagine a small ant wishing to get a comprehensive view of a painted Japanese dinner-plate. He would succeed if he could get a thimble upright in the middle of the plate, then climb to the top of the thimble and look by turns in every direction. The ant, in that hypothesis, occupies a position similar to that of the man in San Francisco, which represents the saucer, and the palatial dwelling of Mrs Mark Hopkins, on California Street Hill, is the thimble.

The description continues with what this ant/man could see, and concludes, 'it may safely be said that the homes of more than a quarter of a million people within this saucer-like panorama, 50 miles long and 15 wide are distinctly visible from the corner of California and Mason streets, 381 feet above ordinary high tide'.

The rest of the information on the card, written by Muybridge, identifies with precision what the viewer sees in the picture on the reverse, and, finally, Muybridge describes a third panorama: 'I also publish a Panorama from same point of view mounted on cloth, and folded vertically in 14 divisions, each 16 by 24 inches making an extended view of 20 feet long'. The existence of the panorama he describes is a mystery. Muybridge might have made such a work, but if he did, it no longer exists. Or he could have been projecting into the future, anticipating the panorama he would make the following summer, in 1878.

That June, Muybridge returned to the Hopkins tower to make a mammoth-plate panorama: thirteen albumen prints which, mounted on paper and backed by a single linen sheet, stretched to more than 17 feet (5.18 m). For this almost overwhelming enterprise, he rethought both his conception and his technology. He changed to a vertical format and divided the circumference into thirteen rather than eleven equal sections, so there would be none of the overlap that he felt marred the previous year's panorama, where the overlap in two images was quite visible. Starting again at about eleven in the morning, and with an as yet unidentified assistant, Muybridge worked at an extraordinary speed, exposing all the 24 x 20-inch (61 x 50.8 cm) negatives as quickly as he had the smaller plates the year before, over a four- to five-hour period. The work went smoothly enough until the seventh view. Some damage occurred, and he had to retake the negative. We can tell this from the different raking of the shadows.

The result was a kind of panorama that had never been seen before; it seemed to obliterate the physical and temporal boundaries of the individual photographic plates while imposing its own challenges to viewing. There is no record of how Muybridge meant

Panorama of San Francisco, 1878, panel 2.

for it to be viewed, whether placed in some contrivance so that it would encircle the viewer at eye level or rolled from one reel to another, like the earlier painted panoramas. The fact that he mounted each photograph and backed it so that it would accordion fold suggests that he probably intended it to be placed on a stand or laid flat on a table.

Once more the facts presented to the camera differ from how the viewer experiences them. Laid out flat, the panorama is a 17-foot-long (5.18 m) ribbon whose length demands that it be seen in increments. The viewer must stop and start, focus on one detail or section and then move on. This effect is emphasized by the height from which Muybridge took the pictures. The viewer lacks a foreground with which to orient him or herself, although Muybridge has compensated for this by relying on the broad lines of the four

Panorama of San Francisco, 1878, panel 3.

streets surrounding the Hopkins site to structure the image. Each
of these streets is seen twice; but instead of forming a continuous
line, they 'appear separate and disconnected in the photographs,
requiring an act of imagination to see them as one and the same'.[17]
With this saccadic movement of the eyes and the body, the viewer
would experience, or re-experience, an extended, completely
subjective moment.

Muybridge's 1878 mammoth-plate panorama was an aesthetic
and technical triumph. He printed nine copies, but never advertised
them. He didn't have the opportunity; the new work for Stanford
was taking up all his time and energy. He did present a copy each
to Jane Stanford and Mary Hopkins (Mark Hopkins had died in
the spring of 1878), and in May 1881 he gave another to Frank Shay.
One other remained with Muybridge until his death.[18]

The advertisement on the back of Muybridge's 1877 key had included a reference to his work photographing horses 'while running at full speed'. The picture in question was of Stanford's horse 'Occident', which Muybridge had made in Sacramento in July of that year and sent to the *Alta California* on 2 August. As the newspaper recounted:

Mr Muybridge sends us a copy of an instantaneous photograph of 'Occident' taken when he was trotting at a speed of 36 feet per second, or a mile in 2 minutes and 27 seconds. The negative was exposed to the light less than one-thousandth part of a second, so brief a time that the horse did not move a quarter of an inch. The photographer had made many experiments to secure the highest sensitiveness and the briefest possible exposure, and the result was a novelty in photographic art, and a delineation of speed which the eye cannot catch.[19]

A letter from Muybridge to the *Alta* accompanying this astonishing photograph and published with the description on 3 August claimed that

the length of exposure can be pretty accurately determined by the fact that the whip in the driver's hand did not move the distance of its diameter. The picture has been retouched as is customary at this time with all first-class photographic work, for the purpose of giving a better effect to the details. In every other respect, the photograph is exactly as it was made in the camera.

The image was reported in the *Bulletin* as well, where on 3 August it was described as a 'triumph of photographic art'. But neither paper published it. Not that photographs could be printed in the press before the advent of the halftone process in 1882, but

'"Occident". Owned by Leland Stanford. Driven by Jas. Tennant. Photographed by Muybridge in less than one-thousandth part of a second, while the horse was trotting at the rate of thirty-six feet per second', cabinet card ('Automatic Electro-Photograph'), 1877.

they were often reproduced as engravings – Muybridge's Modoc War photographs and his images of Guatemala both found their way as engravings into national magazines. And in just a few months, Muybridge would make instantaneous pictures of horses that would be illustrated in the press of almost every country in the world. That no engraving made from this picture of 'Occident' seems to survive, suggests that no print was ever made from the negative. Perhaps that is why, in his letter to the *Alta*, Muybridge invited the editors to his studio to see the negative – not a positive – and the written testimony of the driver as to the speed of the horse.

Yet Muybridge did publish a picture of 'Occident' on a 5 x 7-inch (12.7 x 17.8 cm) card, calling it an 'Automatic Electro-Photograph'. Below the picture he printed:

'Occident', owned by Leland Stanford, trotting at a 2:30 gait over the Sacramento track, in July, 1877. The exposure of the original negative of this photograph was less than the two-thousandth part of a second. The details have been retouched. In this position the horse is entirely clear of the ground, but just about to alight.

Muybridge had retouched both his negatives and prints to add atmosphere or to eliminate elements that intruded into the composition he desired to convey. It was a completely respectable procedure in his day. His retouched 'Occident' led to controversy. On 3 August 'Rambling Writer' of the San Francisco *Post* – the newspaper that had once employed Larkyns – claimed that Muybridge had gone too far:

> Let us look at this triumph of an art seemingly in its infancy:
> The driver, Mr Tennant – I presume it is Mr Tennant though
> I do not enjoy the gentleman's acquaintance – is not driving
> a horse; he is sitting for his photograph. He is stiff, unnatural;
> he does not encourage his horse; he would lean forward were
> he driving at the rate of 36 feet per second; he would be alive
> with movement and the 'hie yar' would, as it were, ring in
> our ears . . . Decidedly, Mr Tennant, you were not driving
> Occident at the rate of 36 feet per second when you sat for
> that photo . . . And here's the rub. Either that camera did
> lie, or Stanford has got the most extraordinary horse in the
> world . . . and he can make more money by exhibiting it than
> by trotting it.

In fact, as we know now, Muybridge had photographed a watercolour by John Koch, the retoucher at Morse's Gallery. The face of the driver is the only camera-made image in Muybridge's 'photograph', and since the painting still exists at the Cantor Arts Center at Stanford University, we also know that the photograph of Tennant's face was glued to the picture before Muybridge photographed it. Muybridge could be accused of perpetrating a hoax, but that would be imposing a very modern conception of just what a photograph is. He had captured an image of 'Occident' and the negative was probably not good enough to make a sale-able print. It was good enough, however, to be the basis of a painting – the negative, or a transparency made from it, would have been projected onto a canvas by a magic lantern, its outlines then traced and the details filled in. While the camera image was a form of proof, the painting made from it would give it a height-ened visibility by adding detail that the camera could not yet capture. At the time, such improvements were totally acceptable.

Apart from 'Rambling Writer', no one else questioned the veracity of Muybridge's photograph. Indeed, the impossibility of the position frozen by the camera was taken to be a sign of the photograph's accuracy. Rather than rendering any notion of the horse's speed, the picture, according to a reporter from the San Francisco *Call*, 'has more the appearance of a sudden stop from motion than the reverse, and many have argued that it could not be taken as represented. Had an artist desired to exemplify speed, he would never have shown a horse in the attitude the photograph displays, and this is the best possible proof of its correctness'.

The writer goes on to claim that 'the countenance of the animal' is the only aspect of the picture to convey movement. 'His ears are thrown back, and the whole face is suffused with determination, while the projecting limbs look as though the effort was to come to an instantaneous halt.'[20] What suggests motion to the reporter, in other words, is the part of the picture in which Koch has taken the most artistic liberty in adding details. The pose of the horse, taken from the photograph, on the other hand, appears false. The truth of the artist and the truth revealed by the camera are at odds. They would be for some time to come.

As the image of 'Occident' was circulating, Muybridge and Stanford were ready to expand the experiments. The description of the photograph in the *Alta California* indicated the direction of their research: 'Mr Muybridge intends to take a series of pictures, showing the step of 'Occident' at all its stages.' On 11 August the paper described in greater detail what the two men were planning:

> Mr Muybridge has now received his instructions and will commence his work as soon as he can receive the needed lenses from London and can have some machinery made here . . . Mr Muybridge will have a dozen photographic cameras placed at intervals of two feet . . . The shutters of these cameras will be opened and shut by electricity as the horse passes in front of each, the time of exposure being as before not more than the thousandth part of a second . . . Each picture will be taken by a double lens so as to be adapted for the stereoscope, and will thus furnish the most conclusive proof to connoisseurs that it is faithfully taken by photography and not materially changed by retouching.

This new work would be carried out at Stanford's new ranch in Palo Alto, and it would result in a new role for the photographer as an investigator of animal locomotion, a role which would make Muybridge famous not just in California, but worldwide.

6

Stopping Time on Stanford's Ranch

In 1874 Stanford had read a book called *Animal Mechanism: A Treatise on Terrestrial and Aerial Locomotion* by the French physiologist Étienne-Jules Marey (who was born and died in the very same years as Muybridge and happened also to share his initials).

Animal Mechanism, translated from the French text published the year before, was a summary of Marey's work on movement, begun in the 1860s. A physiologist interested in mechanics – today we would call him a biophysicist – Marey believed that he could determine the laws underlying the functions of the body, such as the beating of the heart or the mechanics of walking, by using machines to trace them out in the form of graphs. His idea was based on his understanding, rare in France at the time, that the body itself was a machine, one that consumed fuel and expended energy – a motor, in fact, whose functions could be reduced to the newly discovered (1847) laws of thermodynamics.

Marey's great achievement was his adaptation of the graphing machines used in physics to record the body's internal dynamic and external kinetics. In every case, the movement made its own tracings, without recourse to the hand or eye, through instruments Marey created.

Around 1870, Marey began to focus on graphing the phenomena that produce locomotion. He invented some ingenious methods for tracing movement, including special shoes containing a chamber that was connected by rubber tubing to a small, hollow metal drum with a thin skin of rubber stretched across it. This 'tambour' was in turn attached to a stylus that moved over a rotating cylinder covered with smoke-blackened paper. Each movement of the foot was conveyed to the receiving tambour and stylus, registering the number, length and frequency of steps as well as variations of foot pressure on the ground. With some adjustments, this technique also worked for horses.

For Marey, there was 'scarcely any branch of animal mechanics which has given rise to more labour and greater controversy than the question of the paces of the horse', and he described his experiments in some detail. Instead of a hollow-chambered shoe, he attached 'a ball of India-rubber filled with horsehair . . . to the horse's hoof by a contrivance which adapts it to the shoe . . . When the foot strikes the ground, the India-rubber ball is compressed, and drives a part of the confined air into the registering instruments'.[1]

Marey transcribed the traces made by the horse to create what he called his 'synoptical notations'. He then had French Army horseman Colonel Émile Duhousset translate the notations into drawings and published them and the inscriptions in *Animal Mechanism*. They showed that in the trot and the gallop, there was a moment when the animal had all four legs off the ground and was suspended in the air. Marey's research provided the answer to the unsupported transit controversy, but Stanford wanted proof in the form of a photograph, a picture made by a camera – 'the machine that could not lie'.

In the pages of *Animal Mechanism*, Marey also proposed the direction of the new experiments that Stanford would undertake with Muybridge:

Everyone knows the ingenious optical instrument invented by Plateau and called by him 'Phenakistoscope'. This instrument, which is also known by the name of Zootrope [*sic*], resends to the eye a series of successive images of persons or animals represented in various attitudes. When these attitudes are coordinated so as to bring before the eye all the phases of movement, the illusion is complete; we seem to see living persons moving in different ways.

This instrument, usually constructed for the amusement of children, generally represents grotesque or fantastic figures moving in a ridiculous manner. But it has occurred to us that, by depicting on the apparatus figures constructed with care, and representing faithfully the successive attitudes of the body during walking, running, etc., we might reproduce the appearance of the different kinds of progression employed by man.[2]

Further on, Marey describes how Mathias Duval, a professor of anatomy at the École des Beaux-Arts in Paris, had made a series of sixteen pictures of the horse for a zoetrope from Marey and Duhousset's notations and drawings in order to verify their accuracy:

These figures, when placed in the instrument, make the illusion complete, and show us a horse which ambles, walks, or trots as the case may be. Then, if we regulate the swiftness of the rotation given to the instrument, we render the movements which the animal seems to execute more or less rapid, which will permit the inexperienced observer to follow the series of positions of each kind of pace, and soon enable him to distinguish with the eye a series of movements in the living animal which appear at first sight to be in absolute confusion.[3]

Animal Mechanism was the inspiration for the next phase of Stanford's research, a systematic investigation of the gaits of the horse through a *series* of photographs that, reconstituted in a zoetrope, would give him the evidence he needed both to breed and to train his stable of horses. Stanford was in a unique position to carry out the endeavour. In addition to having the great wealth to fund the experiments, he had the ideal place to carry them out: in 1876, as Muybridge was photographing Stanford's mansion in San Francisco, his patron purchased the 650-acre Mayfield Grange, 35 miles south of the city, near Menlo Park. There, Stanford built a country house for his family, and over the following years bought up neighbouring farms until he had amassed around 8,000 acres. He named it the Palo Alto Stock Farm, after a redwood tree on the banks of San Francisquito Creek, and developed one of the finest experimental horse breeding and training centres in the country.

When Stanford invited Muybridge to renew his experiments in photographing his horses, the photographer was reluctant at first. 'Personally, I would as soon execute the work at Sacramento as at Palo Alto', he wrote to Stanford's assistant Alfred Poett, 'were I assured that I would not be interfered with by people exercising horses and others of the public'. But in the same letter he wrote that he had 'written to the Governor at Palo Alto suggesting that we make the series of photos illustrating the stride of a trotting horse, at Palo Alto, instead of at Sacramento . . . If the Governor decided to have me come to Palo Alto, I would like to see you before you lay out a track as there are many things to be considered necessary for perfect success'.[4]

Making instantaneous photographs – that is, photographs with an exposure time of less than half a second – was virtually impossible with the cumbersome wet-plate process, although a few photographers had certainly succeeded. As early as the mid-1850s, Gustave Le Gray, a French photographer who shared Muybridge's technical virtuosity as well as his taste for photographing water and for combination printing, had developed a technique for 'freezing' ocean waves as they crashed on rocks or lapped the shore. Other photographers, including Adolphe Braun and George Washington Wilson, had captured passers-by on the streets of Paris and Edin-burgh, respectively, by taking the pictures from a distance and using a smaller camera. The awkward positions such photographs revealed, however, were quite different from anything ever seen or represented by artists.

In two pictures that Muybridge made of coffee being loaded onto ships in Guatemala in 1875 he also had frozen the movement of waves lapping the shore; even then, he had already been thinking about capturing movement. In the *Bulletin* on 3 August 1877, he recalled that during his trip to Central America he had experimented with photographing scenes on shore from a rolling ship. The experiments, he said, 'resulted in the construction of an apparatus and the preparation of chemicals so as to permit the photographing in outline of a rapidly moving body'. But just as with his photograph of 'Occident' in 1877, all of these attempts met with only sporadic success. It took considerable ingenuity to make the wet plate produce an instantaneous image. And Stanford and Muybridge proposed to make not just one image, but a series of them. To achieve their goal, they would have to rethink almost every aspect of the medium.

They started with the cameras, twelve of them in all.[5] Stereo cameras were chosen because their backs were closer to the lenses, which, along with their size, allowed more light to reach the plate. Muybridge ordered the cameras from the Scovill Company of New York and the lenses from Dallmeyer in London. They then needed to rethink the shutters, which is where Muybridge's technical ingenuity came into play. There were no built-in camera shutters when Muybridge was making photographs. To expose a plate and make an image, the photographer would remove the lens cap, count off the seconds, and then replace the cap. Even though a skilled photographer knew, from years of practice, just how long to expose the plate – based on weather, time of day and other conditions – Muybridge was aiming for an exposure in the range of a thousandth of a second. This demanded a mechanical, not human action; he also needed a method for triggering the twelve shutters sequentially as well as remotely.

Muybridge started experimenting with a shutter made of two small, horizontal wooden slats with a space between them through which the light could hit the plate behind the lens. A strong rubber band snapped the slats up and down, masking, demasking and once again masking the lens. In his final version of the device, he added a second shutter, identical to the first, that moved in the opposite direction reducing the exposure time even more.

To trigger the shutters, he used electricity. Stanford had delegated his chief engineer, Samuel S. Montague, to help Muybridge create the shutters, based on sketches the photographer had made. Montague in turn sent Muybridge to Arthur Brown, superintendent of bridges and buildings in Oakland. Brown put his carpenters to work on constructing the shutters according to Muybridge's specifications, and invited a young engineer named John D. Isaacs to help figure out how to operate them. Isaacs later described a discussion he had about Muybridge's drawings with one Mr Palmer, in which they

> came to the conclusion that no mechanical contrivance of sufficient delicacy and rapidity to accomplish the purpose could be devised. We did not believe it could be done and we had just about concluded our conversation on the subject and I think Mr Palmer was about to change the subject when I said 'I have got it sir; it is electricity', and the details of the whole thing just flashed into my mind in an instant. I thought of putting a magnet on the outside of the apparatus to pull out a catch, connecting that magnet with a battery on one side and with a wire which should reach over the track with the other; also connecting the battery with another wire which should run over the track and lie parallel with the first wire.[6]

Isaacs's report of his 'eureka' moment has raised questions about whose idea it was to use electricity to trigger the shutters.

Camera shutters, from Muybridge's album of original photographs, *The Attitudes of Animals in Motion . . .* , 1881.

His account is taken from his testimony in a lawsuit that Muybridge launched against Stanford in 1885 over the publication of the Palo Alto photographs. In another record of testimony, Charles Knowles, one of the carpenters assigned to construct the shutters, reports the following conversation when Muybridge came to see how the work was going. 'Knowles: "It was a very happy thought of Isaacs in suggesting electricity for working this apparatus for getting instantaneous pictures by having a series of shutters or slides to work up and down as the horse passes in front." Muybridge: "Yes, it was a very bright thought . . . Moreover it is going to revolutionize photography."'[7]

And yet there is also evidence that Muybridge devised the electrical triggers on his own. We do know that while purchasing supplies with Poett in San Francisco in September 1877, Muybridge had gone to the Electrical Construction House, and on 11 October he wrote to Poett, 'I would like to . . . show you the apparatus and electrical machines I am having constructed and which are very nearly finished'.[8] On 3 November he bought $130 dollars of 'Electrical Photo apparatus' from the San Francisco Telegraph Supply Company, the maker, according to a newspaper report, of the electrical portion of the appliances.[9] Muybridge had named

Camera shutters, from *The Attitudes of Animals in Motion . . .* , 1881.

his earlier photograph of 'Occident' an 'Automatic Electro-Photograph', suggesting that he had already grasped the part that electricity would play in the work. And finally, Muybridge quickly patented the shutter apparatus, including its electrical elements, without any protest from Stanford.

With cameras and shutters taken care of, the next element was to create a space in which the horses could be photographed at the speed Muybridge proposed. First, there needed to be a place to house the twelve cameras. Directed by Muybridge, the farmhands and carpenters constructed a building alongside the mile-long track used for training Stanford's trotters. This shed had a low 50-foot-long (15.2 m) counter on which Muybridge placed the cameras at 21-inch (53 cm) intervals. The cameras faced a whitewashed 'screen of planks' opposite. This screen was 15 feet

(4.57 m) high, angled away from the cameras at about 70 degrees, and marked with vertical lines at 21-inch (53 cm) – and in three cases 27-inch (68 cm) – intervals and numbers from one to twenty painted between each line. On the ground was angled another four-plank barrier with horizontal lines painted at 4-inch (10 cm) intervals; it was used to measure the height attained by the hooves. In front of this barrier was a strip of wood fastened to the ground into which grooves had been cut to set a spring-loaded wire corresponding to the lines on the background, 'so arranged that when the wire crossing the track was depressed by the wheel it should draw upon the spring connected with it, and make contact with a metallic button and complete the electric circuit'.[10] The track itself was covered by lime – calcium carbonate – ground from limestone or marble that made it as white as snow. Everything was white, to get the highest contrast possible.

Finally, while the new shutters, their electromagnetic triggering, the brilliant whiteness of the track and the white wall behind the horses were each critical elements in the successful production of the images, perhaps the most important, as photography historian Joel Snyder has observed, was Muybridge's use of an ammoniac developer that made the collodion effectively more light sensitive.[11] (An exchange in the March 1879 *Philadelphia Photographer*, in which Muybridge declined to disclose the details of his method – and in particular the chemicals he used – supports this view.)

Once the track and shed were completed in May 1878, the experiments began. After preliminary run-throughs on 9 and 11 June, for which a *Bulletin* reporter was present, Stanford invited a larger press contingent, his friends and disinterested turfmen to the ranch on 15 June to witness the entire process: to watch each horse run over the glaring white track in front of the cameras and then to view in the darkroom the sequence of negatives that had captured what they had seen – or actually, had not seen nor could ever see – as Muybridge developed and fixed each one.

The presence of the media at the demonstration was important in part to preclude the type of criticism that had been levelled against the photograph/painting of 'Occident' published the year before. Muybridge's single photograph of Koch's painting had been praised for the energy of the animal's face and damned for the position of its body – the face conformed to what could be seen and was in line with what viewers expected, while the body looked wrong, showing what could be 'seen' only by a camera. More photographic evidence was needed to confirm the body's position. Indeed, according to one report, the series of photographs that Muybridge undertook were made precisely because the single photograph 'so misrepresented the position of the horse in the minds of even experienced turfmen, that the artist decided to make his next experiments on a principle which would certainly carry conviction to even the most incredulous natures'.[12]

With the press assembled, the trotter 'Abe Edgington', driven by Stanford's chief trainer, Charles Marvin, raced along the track. As planned, the metal wheels of the carriage rolled over the wires, completing each electric circuit and tripping the shutters. 'Abe Edgington' was followed by a mare, 'Sallie Gardner', and her jockey. Rather than triggering the shutters electrically, 'Sallie Gardner' tripped them manually by breaking strings that had been stretched across her path. Spooked by her repeated bumping into the strings as she ran, after breaking the eighth or ninth, she 'gave a wild bound in the air, breaking the saddle girth as she left the ground'.[13] The accident was caught in the negatives, soon viewed by the invited guests. Watched over by the reporters who accompanied him to the darkroom at the far end of the camera shed, Muybridge developed and presented the exposed negatives within twenty minutes of their being taken. The onlookers were overwhelmed: 'There is a feeling of awe in the mind of the beholder, as he looks at the glass plate which is held before the yellow curtain, and he sees the miniature of the nying [sic] horse so perfect that it startles him. . . . It is a new era in photography and instantaneous is no longer a misnomer.'[14]

Within a few days, the miracle of what had occurred was reported in every local newspaper. In the *Sacramento Daily Union* on 18 June, the writer celebrated the accomplishment:

> The feat performed by Muybridge, an artist of this coast . . . is second only, among the marvels of the age, to the wonderful discoveries of the telephone and phonograph. . . . The negatives were very small, but perfect in outline and detail even to showing the shape of each spoke in the wheel . . . These pictures, which could not be otherwise than true, prove that the horse in trotting assumes positions never dreamed of before – positions which, while they rob the horse of that gracefulness generally credited to him when going at full speed, the knowledge of which will nevertheless prove invaluable to persons concerned in the care and training of trotters. They show the legs to be in almost all conceivable positions.

This report, and most of what would soon follow, insisted on the accuracy of the photographs in the face of the near belief that photographs could only depict what anyone could see in front of the camera. Muybridge's high-speed photographs demonstrated a new actuality: photography could represent aspects of the world in motion that were beyond the capacity of human visible perception, and the technologically precise and repeatable manner in which they were produced made the unexpected, graceless pictures irrefutable.

For the *Sacramento Daily Union* reporter, there was no conflict in an artist such as Muybridge, who had fashioned his career by depicting what the eye could see, using his art to capture what the eye could not see. The demonstration for the press made it clear that even though the photographs robbed the horse of its gracefulness and depicted it in ungainly positions, they revealed an inviolate

THE HOR

Patent for apparatus applied for.   M U

"SALLIE GARDNER," owned by **LELAND STANFORD**; ridden

The negatives of these photographs were made at intervals of twenty-seven inches o
during a single stride of the mare.   The vertical lines were twent
The negatives were each exposed during the tw

The Horse in Motion – 'Sallie Gardner', 'owned by Leland Stanford; ridden by
G. Domm; running at a 1.40 gait over the Palo Alto track, 19th June 1878'.

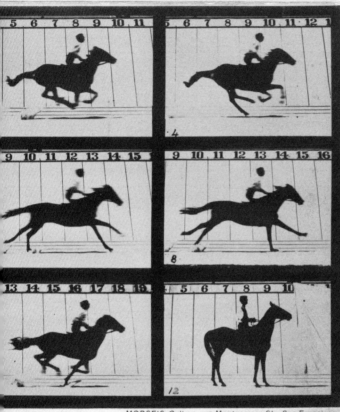

Motion.

E.

AUTOMATIC ELECTRO-PHOTOGRAPH.

IM, running at a 1.40 gait over the Palo Alto track, 19th June, 1878.

out the twenty-fifth part of a second of time; they illustrate consecutive positions assumed
art; the horizontal lines represent elevations of four inches each.
of a second, and are absolutely "untouched."

truth of some kind. Muybridge's method 'precluded all suspicion of mistakes, and insured accuracy which could not be questioned'.[15]

But there were dissenters. In the August issue of the *Philadelphia Photographer*, William Rulofson decried the results 'as diminutive silhouettes of the animal on and against a white background or wall . . . Photographically speaking, it is "bosh"; but then it amused the "boys", and shows that a horse trots part of the time and "flies" the rest, a fact of "utmost scientific importance". Bosh again'. Poor Rulofson. The previous February, Muybridge had taken him to court demanding $5,000 in damages for destroying four of his Yosemite negatives and damaging 21 others. Muybridge testified that he had mortgaged the negatives in order to borrow money from the firm in 1872; Rulofson claimed he had bought the negatives outright and Muybridge was owed nothing. On 2 November 1878, with the suit still not settled, Rulofson fell to his death from the roof of his gallery while examining a new skylight. Shortly thereafter, in its November issue, the editor of the *Philadelphia Photographer* countered Rulofson's criticism by analysing the photographs and asserting that he could not have given much thought to the subject in reaching his conclusions: 'Mr Muybridge deserves great credit, and has gained great notoriety for what he has done, and we shall try to induce him sometime to tell us more about it'.

The press gave Muybridge and Stanford equal praise for the brilliant success:

It is difficult to say to whom we should award the greater praise, Governor Stanford, for the inception of an idea so original and for the liberality with which he has supplied the funds for such a costly experiment, or to Muybridge for the energy, genius and devotion with which he has pursued his experiments and so successfully overcome all the scientific, chemical and mechanical difficulties encountered in labors which had no precedent, and which have so happily culminated in such a wonderful result.[16]

Attainable only through the combination of Stanford's money and Muybridge's technical ingenuity – made practical, in turn, by Stanford's engineers – the 'wonderful result' confirmed Stanford's reputation and established Muybridge's. Stanford's reward would be to increase the public perception of him as a philanthropist interested in the higher good, and not just as a railroad baron whose role in the completion of the transcontinental railroad – a towering accomplishment over almost insurmountable odds – forever tied him to the physical embodiment of Manifest Destiny. The perception was that Stanford, by engaging Muybridge, was making a valuable contribution to science and, more important, considering that the hallmark of science was its association with mechanical objectivity, he was doing it through mechanization. The fact that it was a machine that supplied the proof – that the 'horse took his own picture', as the *California Spirit of the Times* proclaimed on 22 June – gave a gloss of modernity and progress to the project and, by association, to Stanford himself.

For his part, Muybridge became a celebrity, first locally and then worldwide. The press already considered him to be 'an artist of rare skill', but now they accorded him new status as 'a photographer of genius'.[17] One reporter expressed the hope that Muybridge would 'reap the benefits to which his genius and success clearly entitled him',[18] and the photographer was not slow to do so.

Although the outcome of the experiments was attributed in the press to a collaborative process, we know from a receipt for payment for drawings and specifications that Muybridge had begun making plans to patent his shutters and the track arrangement as early as 14 June.[19] On 27 June he applied for a patent on an 'Apparatus for Photographing Objects in Motion' and on 11 July submitted another application on the same subject. The first covered the background, the camera shutters and the electrical system needed to operate them, while the second covered the mechanical operation of the shutters by the horse breaking the strings. Both patents were issued on 4 March 1879. French, German and British patents followed.

Next Muybridge copyrighted a series of cabinet cards and published them through Morse's Gallery. In the prototype, titled *The Stride of a Trotting Horse*, Muybridge affixed twelve 1 x 1¾-inch (2.54 x 4.45 cm) prints of 'Abe Edgington', arranged in three rows of four images per row, onto a preprinted card, awaiting the borders of black tape that would be added before the whole thing was re-photographed in a single image. The preprinted legend below the pictures identifies the name of the horse, the day (11 June), the gait (2.24), and the exposure time ('about the two-thousandth part of a second') and explains that 'the vertical lines were placed 21 inches apart, and the horizontal lines represent elevations of 4, 8 and 12 inches, respectively, above the level of the track'. The phrase 'Automatic Electro-Photograph by Muybridge' stands out in bold letters on the right. On the left 'Copyright, 1878' and 'Patent for apparatus applied for' completes the information.

In the final version – a series of six cards called *The Horse in Motion*, reverting to the title used for the photograph of 'Occident' painted by Koch – black borders separate each picture in the sequence and the phrase 'The negatives are absolutely "untouched"' was added to each card. A close look at the photographs, however, reveals that Muybridge's claim needs to be taken with a grain of salt. While the negatives might not have been retouched, the prints are another story. Muybridge retouched when he needed to – outlining the legs, mouth or mane of the horse; highlighting the midtones; and de-emphasizing the background. Such retouching is most clearly evident in the picture of 'Abe Edgington': in each of the twelve images, the jockey has been painted over to make a silhouette.

The Horse in Motion was published as a series, one card for $2.50 and $15 for all six (besides 'Abe Edgington' and 'Sallie Gardner', Muybridge had photographed the horses 'Mahomet' and 'Occident'). Each card illustrates a 'single stride', but not every one is made up of twelve images. 'Sallie Gardner's 19 June run 'at a 1:40 gait' was captured in eleven photographs; 'Abe Edgington' 'trotting at an 8 minute gait' in eight and 'walking at a 15 minute gait' on 18 June in six. There were also only six images of 'Mahomet', cantering at an eight-minute gait. In order to fit these disparate groupings of images (including twelve each of 'Abe Edgington' and 'Occident' trotting on 15 June and on 20 June, respectively) onto the same 4 × 8 (10.8 × 21 cm) cards, however, Muybridge had to be resourceful in the way he printed his sequences. The card showing the six phases of 'Mahomet's canter, for example, is arranged in two rows of three pictures, with thicker borders around each image and between the rows than in other cards. To 'Sallie Gardner's eleven images Muybridge added a twelfth picture of a horse and rider at rest. Such creativity in organizing his sequences would become a hallmark of his work in Philadelphia less than a decade later.

The back of the cards again contained supplemental information. Two-thirds of the space was given over to a description of the position of the limbs in each image and an analysis of the stride, probably written by Stanford. The bottom third listed Muybridge's name, 'Landscape and Animal Photographer', his designation as official photographer and grand prize medallist winner, and then also his new role: *Inventor and Patentee in the United States, England, France, etc. of the Automatic Electro-Photographic Apparatus*. The cards were published in France and Germany as well as the United States and Britain.

Though not included on the cards, Muybridge was also recognized by this time as a gifted lecturer. As early as 1872, he had given public presentations of his photographs in the form of glass slides projected by a magic lantern, accompanied by explanations, descriptions, and riveting tales of his adventures in Yosemite, at the Lava Beds and in Central America. Like the popular travel lecture, Muybridge's demonstrations placed himself and his exploits at the centre of a narrative illustrated by the slides, which he projected using dissolves, cut-ins, exterior/interior and point-of-view shots that heralded similar editing techniques in cinema.[20] Muybridge's lectures appealed to the same middle-class audience that took such delight in his stereos and panoramas. Such entertainments, part of a larger family that included wax museums, expositions and department store displays, produced their visual pleasure by transforming the real world into spectacular images for mass consumption.[21]

On 8 July 1878 before an astonished audience at the San Francisco Art Association, Muybridge presented his pictures of Stanford's horses, adding scientific lecturer to his many roles. As its name implies, the scientific lecture had a more educational aim, that of popularizing contemporary discoveries and conveying in a palatable fashion basic scientific principles to an untutored public. As the *Chronicle* reported the next day: 'The attendance was not so large as might have been expected, considering the unique manner in which the illustrations were described', but the 'strange attitudes assumed by each animal excited much comment and surprise, so different were they from those pictures representing our famous trotters at their full stride. But that which still more aroused astonishment and mirth, was the action of the racer at full gallop . . . so complex and ungraceful were many of the positions, where on the race track beauty, elegance and symmetry are all so combined'. Muybridge completed the evening with a 'pretty set of pictures delineating life and scenes in Central America, concluding with a perfect panorama of San Francisco and the surrounding country'. He showed himself to be 'a clever and lucid lecturer on a very difficult subject, while his remarks on the Central America series were humorous and excelled in descriptive powers'.

A charismatic lecturer, Muybridge was also an accomplished lanternist, able to show the trotting and racing horses in a sequence fast enough to permit the audience to visualize the phases of their movement as a continuum. At the August San Francisco Mechanics' Fair, according to the *Bulletin* of 28 August 1878, he projected pictures of 'Abe Edgington' and 'Occident' on a 'large screen in the waiting-room adjoining the cloak-rooms, by the aid of calcium light', commenting on them as they 'pass[ed] in quick succession before the gaze of the observer'. The exhibition would take place each night, the reporter explained, and dispelled 'into thin air . . . the false theories concerning the movements of a trotter while in rapid motion. The action of the trotter in motion as caught by the camera is very different to what the artist usually makes it appear on canvas. Not since the time of the Egyptians, as Mr Muybridge remarks, has the animal been delineated as he appears in these negatives [*sic*]'.

Based on comparisons made in Duhousset's 1874 book *Le Cheval* (The Horse), which the Colonel had dedicated to artists, Muybridge's demonstrations of the contrast between artist's renderings of the horse's movements and those captured by the camera was the basis of lectures he would give until the end of his life. During the week of 10 September 1878 Muybridge perfected his lecturing skills with presentations at the Art Association, and on 19 September, at the Congregational Church in Sacramento, he showed not just the horses but also one hundred of the Central America series.

News of Muybridge's triumph rapidly spread beyond the local press. On 23 June the *New York Times* had carried the *Bulletin*'s report, and in July the photographs of 'Sallie Gardner' appeared in the *Photographic News* in London. In October *Scientific American* dedicated its front page to a sequence of engravings made from the photographs – but without the jockey – and suggested they be mounted in a zoetrope to verify their accuracy, since the 'conventional figure of a trotting horse in motion does not appear in any of [the photographs] nor anything like it'.[22]

On 14 December the sequences of 'Abe Edgington' trotting and 'Sallie Gardner' galloping were published as engravings in *La Nature*, the French journal of popular science. ('Sallie Gardner's jockey, rendered as a total silhouette in Muybridge's cabinet card, wears a light-coloured shirt in the engraving.) Marey's response, published in a letter to the journal's editor, Gaston Tissandier, four days later, expresses their importance for both science and art and reiterates the possibility of their synthesis in the zoetrope:

> Dear Friend, I am filled with admiration for Mr Muybridge's instantaneous photographs . . . Could you put me in touch with the author? I would like to ask him to assist in the solution of certain physiological problems so difficult to resolve by other methods. For instance on the question of the flight of birds, I was dreaming of a kind of *photographic gun*, to seize the bird in a pose, or, even better, in a series of poses marking the successive phases of the movement of its wings . . . It is clearly an easy experiment for Mr Muybridge. And then what beautiful zoetropes he will be able to give us: in them we will see all imaginable animals in their true paces; it will be animated zoology. As for artists, it is a revolution, since they will be provided with the true attitudes of movement, those positions of the body in unstable balance for which no model can *pose*. You see, my dear friend, my enthusiasm is boundless.[23]

Muybridge replied to Tissandier on 17 February, asking him to assure Marey of his 'high regard' and to tell him that the 'reading of his famous work on animal mechanism first inspired Governor Stanford with the first idea of the possibility of resolving the problem of locomotion with the help of photography'. Muybridge added that although he thought photographing birds in flight would be difficult, he would 'set about it as best we can'.

In this letter, Muybridge also mentions that Stanford had asked him 'to pursue a more complete series of experiments. To this end we have constructed thirty cameras with electric shutters that, for the photography of horses, will be placed about twelve inches from each other. We will begin our experiments next May'.[24]

On 20 November 1878 the *Alta* claimed that Stanford had 'instructed Mr Muybridge to double the number of his cameras'. In the meantime, Muybridge was also making adjustments to his apparatus. One resulted in another patent application for a pneumatic clock with which to regulate the tripping of the shutters. He also made changes to his track, placing a board on the front edge – closest to the camera shed – and marking it off with numbers every twelve inches (30.5 cm). By the spring of 1879 the second battery of twelve cameras was in place for a total of 24 (not 30 as Stanford had suggested). Muybridge had devised a clockwork mechanism to trip the shutters – a cam that rotated through a series of electrical connections – instead of the animals breaking the threads. And he began to expand his subject matter to include various domestic animals. His photographs of greyhounds attracted particular notice in the press because of their potential application in breeding and training, but the pictures of oxen lumbering by and of a pig prodded into action were equally interesting. Finally, in August, he began to photograph members of the Olympic Club, founded by his old publisher Nahl, and to which he himself belonged.

And there, amidst the running, high-jumping, boxing, wrestling, fencing and tumbling athletes, we find Muybridge again. Fully clothed, he appears in two parts of a sequence of fifteen different and artfully arranged images of athletes posing – the 9 August *Chronicle* referred to them as 'various classical groupings'. He tips his hat to the club's strongman, L. Brandt, in the first picture and shakes hands with him in the second, his clothed body rather conspicuous next to Brandt in his loincloth and the rippling muscles of the other all-but-naked men.

Muybridge is naked in one series of himself running and in another of eighteen images, striking poses that evidently were photographed at different times rather than in a strict chronological

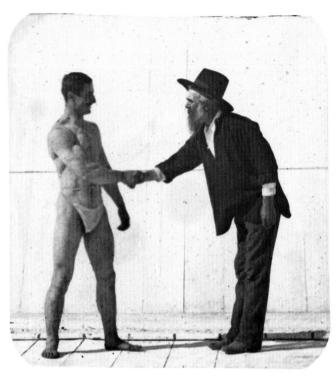

Muybridge posing with San Francisco Olympic Club strongman L. Brandt; lantern slide from an original photograph, 1879.

sequence. He wields a pickaxe, and his movements show off his muscular form; in some of the pictures, he has a pipe in his mouth. The pickaxe seems a curious accessory, but it was an implement familiar to his audience: a tool with which to farm, to mine and even to bring the railroad across the country.

Also in August, Muybridge devised a new camera arrangement for photographing the athletes. Instead of having the cameras parallel to the subject operate in sequence, he placed four, or five or six of them in a semicircle around the subject and triggered their shutters simultaneously. The result – he called them foreshortenings

– was a single figure or pose seen from four or more viewpoints, as if one were walking around it; in modern parlance, we call this a tracking shot, but here it was mapped out on a flat surface. These tracking shots extend duration, but in a way that differs from the panorama. In the tracking shots, it is the subject, not the camera, that seems to pivot, while the viewer remains fixed. And whereas the panorama records an extension of time measured in hours, the tracking shots present everything you can see in a split second, from multiple points of view all at the same time.

Muybridge probably invented the arrangement at the suggestion of an artist called Mr Perry, who wanted a 'quartering view' to assist him in making a painting of a coach and four horses. In his 'classical groupings' of athletes and in these new tracking shots, in particular, Muybridge realized Marey's proposal that the camera would be helpful to artists because it could be used to freeze unstable positions that the eye could not see; the advantage of the tracking shots was that they could do so from three dimensions.

Artists had already been quick to respond to the publication of the photographs. The American painter Thomas Eakins had written to Muybridge in November 1878, after the publication of the cabinet cards. Eakins had disliked the lines on the wall behind the horse, and explained the difficulties they posed for him: 'The lines being further off than the horse a calculation was necessary to establish the size of your measure. The horses being a little nearer or a little farther from the reflecting screen deranged and complicated the calculation each time.'[25] Muybridge responded in May, telling Eakins of his new experiments, including another improvement for the track, laying it 'with rubber, painted white, with black stripes corresponding with the vertical lines on the background'.[26] In the meantime, Eakins, together with Fairman Rogers, a wealthy Philadelphia engineer and member of the board of directors of the Philadelphia Academy of the Fine Arts, where Eakins taught, used the photographs to construct trajectories

Muybridge in various poses with a pickaxe, from *The Attitudes of Animals in Motion* 1881.

made by the movement of each leg of the horse and sent them to Muybridge. Eakins also used this diagrammatic analysis to assist in a painting of Rogers's horses and carriage, *A May Morning in the Park* or *The Fairman Rogers Four-in-Hand* (1879).

Other artists and general enthusiasts used Muybridge's cabinet cards and the published engravings of the sequences to make zoetrope strips in order to reconstitute the motion. These included Marey's illustrator Colonel Duhousset, who through the Paris journal *L'Illustration* offered strips made for 10 francs in April 1879; the editor of English journal *The Field*, who in June had given a crowd-pleasing zoetrope demonstration with strips he had made; and Fairman Rogers himself, who discussed the zoetropes he had made in the July issue of the Philadelphia *Art Interchange*.

Rogers claimed that Muybridge and Stanford had made their own zoetrope strips as well, and we know that Muybridge constructed a stereoscopic-zoetropic viewer with which he apparently was able to view his sequences in three dimensions.[27] During the summer of 1879, however, Muybridge was engaged on a much larger scheme to validate his photographs and publicize his triumph. He was working on a machine that would allow him to rapidly project the pictures, vividly re-creating the movements he had captured for large audiences all over the world.

7

Touring Europe

Muybridge combined his magic lantern expertise and zoetrope experiments in a machine he initially named the zoographoscope, then (until 1881) the zoogyroscope, and finally the zoopraxiscope.[1] He had it made to his specifications by the California Electrical Company, showing the prototype at Stanford's home in the fall of 1879. Onto a wall he projected a series of painted silhouettes, each reproducing a single phase of motion captured by his cameras rapidly enough to reconstitute an entire movement. This magical combination of technology, photography and art constitutes Muybridge's contribution to the birth of cinema, the most popular and enduring of the entertainments to emerge from the new technologies of representation and spectacle.

Muybridge's zoopraxiscope was based on the phenakistoscope (the name was obtained from the Greek word for 'trickery' or 'cheating'), which was invented in 1833 by the Belgian physicist J. A. Plateau. A similar instrument, called a stroboscope, was created independently by the Austrian Simon Ritter von Stampfer at about the same time. In both, a cardboard disc bore a series of figures arranged around its circumference, each figure representing one of successive phases of a movement. When placed behind a second, fenestrated disc of the same size, and spun so that each image passed the eye at faster than a tenth of a second, the images drawn on the wheel blended together to give the illusion of continuous fluid movement. Like the zoetrope, the phenakistoscope was

A 1948 replica of the 1880 zoopraxiscope in the Science Museum, London.

one of the many 'philosophical toys' that furnished nineteenth-century parlours.

In 1845 German engineer Franz von Uchatius created the first projecting phenakistoscope. The phases of the movement were hand painted on glass slides set into a disc turned by a crank; the fenestrated disc was made out of metal instead of cardboard, and a magic lantern projected the images onto a wall. At first, Uchatius used an oil lamp, so the projection was weak; but in 1853 he substituted lime-light for oil and replaced the fenestrated disc with individual lenses for each image, all focused on the same spot. Each separate image – there were usually twelve – was arranged in a circular crib, and a crank brought each of them quickly in front of the light source and their proper lens. By the 1850s other models were on sale, including a variation on Uchatius's marketed by the Parisian Louis Duboscq in which the images were incorporated into a rotating disc of lenses.

Muybridge's zoopraxiscope combined a magic lantern, a lens and, between the two, a gearing mechanism that rotated two discs: a glass disc measuring sixteen inches (40.6 cm) in diameter and, turning in the opposite direction, a fenestrated metal-shutter disc. The glass disc bore figures around its circumference, illustrating 'one or more complete and recurring acts of motion, or a combination of them: for example, an athlete turning a somersault on horseback, while the animal was cantering; a horse making a few strides of the gallop, a leap over a hurdle, another few strides, another leap, and so on; or a group of galloping horses'.[2]

In Muybridge's zoopraxiscope, as in most of the projecting phenakistoscopes that preceded it, the picture disc and slotted shutter disc rotated in opposite directions with an unsettling effect: the figures were distorted, appearing squeezed as well as unnaturally tall and thin. One solution, published in 1869 as the 'Wheel of Life', was to use a shutter disc with only one slot and combine it with a disc bearing thirteen images that would advance by one image each time the shutter disc made a full rotation at great speed. But Muybridge could not use such a mechanism. His large glass discs would simply be too heavy to move at the speed of the 'Wheel of Life'. And Muybridge did not want to be limited to using the same fixed number of images on the circumference of each of his discs; furthermore, he wanted to vary the number of slots on his shutter discs too. Having a shutter disc with the same number of slots as images on the picture disc produced a subject 'running on the spot'. By contrast, more or fewer slots in the shutter allowed the figures to move backward or forward and slower or faster. Muybridge needed this flexibility: he wanted more than just one series of figures to prance and leap before his audience.

A horse and rider, an 1893 zoopraxiscope paper disc adapted from Muybridge's *Animal Locomotion*, 1887.

Muybridge's genius was to combine his figures – the somersaulting Olympic Club athlete with the cantering horse, or individual horses galloping in groups – so his viewers were presented with both variety and narrative. But he had to find a way to compensate for the distortion effects that the rotating discs produced. Using shutters with variable numbers of slots complicated the situation even more. To resolve the problem, he hired an artist to paint the figures as squat and horizontally elongated on the disc; they would then appear normal when projected.[3]

Although Muybridge asserted that the images on the glass discs were retouched photographs, and that in the retouching 'great care was invariably taken to preserve the photographic outline intact',[4] they were in fact painted silhouettes without any photographic image underneath them. Photographic prints of the individual figures, which had been conically bent to distort them and then rephotographed, no doubt were placed under the glass as a guide for overpainting, but no photographic material found its way onto the glass disc. Although an excellent retoucher, Muybridge didn't trust himself to make the paintings. He must have prepared the elongated photographs to guide the painter's hand, but hired an artist to paint the final images.

Muybridge described Stanford's reception of the machine in 'Leland Stanford's Gift to Art and to Science, Mr Muybridge's Inventions of Instant Photography and the Marvelous Zoö-gyroscope', a history of his Palo Alto experiments he wrote but which the *San Francisco Examiner* published anonymously on 6 February 1881:

When Mr Muybridge had achieved success with the zoogyro-scope he had one series of photographs done in silhouette on the outer rim of one glass disc, and with the apparatus hastened to Palo Alto to show the result to Mr Stanford. Across the great screen again and again galloped at full speed a delicate-limbed race mare. Mr Stanford looked at it. 'That is Phryne Lewis' said Mr Muybridge. 'You are mistaken', said Mr Stanford; 'I know the gait too well. That is Florence Anderson'. The artist was certain it was Phryne Lewis. Mr Stanford was equally certain it was Florence Anderson, and it was only after investigation and the discovery that by a misunderstanding it was the pictures of Florence Anderson that had been done in silhouette that the artist was convinced of his error. The series of pictures taken are perfect and numerous, and include those of athletes running, wrestling and turning somersaults.[5]

Stanford's biographers also included the story of mistaken horse identity, although the names of the horses differ. None the less, the story's point is the same: Stanford's recognition of the difference between the two horses was testimony both to his acute powers of observation and to the excellent quality of Muybridge's zoopraxiscope.

On 16 January 1880 Muybridge gave another show for Stanford and some friends, including Charles Crocker and the state governor; he continued these private performances well into March. His zoopraxiscope work did not prevent him, however, from pursuing other experiments. One was a picture of seven stages of the solar eclipse on 11 January 'Photographed for Hon. Leland Stanford at Palo Alto, California, by Muybridge', which combined photographs with hand-painted images on an oval cabinet card. The other was a commission that included Muybridge's only known spirit photographs. An extremely popular genre that played with the 'ghosting' caused by movement when the camera lens was open during a long exposure, spirit photography was a 'photographic recreation' for many, while for nineteenth-century believers in spiritualism and the occult, it was a logical extension of the camera's ability to capture what was invisible to the eye.

The 'ghosts' Muybridge photographed were played by Robert C. Johnson and his wife, Kate, and the photographs were part of 84 that Muybridge made of their residences. The Johnsons had a country house, 'Heartsease', near Stanford's in Menlo Park, and a house in San Francisco, though not on Nob Hill. We don't know how Muybridge and Johnson originally met, but their paths had crossed more than once. Johnson was on the board of the Buena Vista Winery when Muybridge photographed it, and both men

Plate 119 from the Kate and Robert Johnson Photograph Album, 1880.

were in Paris on 3 December 1862 according to that day's *Daily Alta California*.

Unlike his pictures of Stanford's palatial rooms, Muybridge's photographs of the two Johnson residences depict well-lived-in domestic environments. The Johnson rooms are filled with clocks, pictures and mirrors that reappear from one picture to another. Muybridge carefully composed his photographs to achieve specific effects. He shot the exterior of the San Francisco house from a worm's-eye view, giving it the appearance of being atop a hill; he photographed the interiors to include elaborate groupings of paintings and mirrors that reflect their owners: Kate was a painter who specialized in animals, and the couple owned 32 cats. In one of the spirit photographs, Kate lies on a daybed, a photograph of Robert at her feet, and in a double exposure, the ghost of Robert hovers over her. Another double exposure makes Kate the spirit, haunting the room in which Robert is seen reflected in a mirror.

These elaborately staged pictures are the result of a collaboration between Muybridge and the Johnsons, and Muybridge, now an expert in capturing what the eye could not see, must have been delighted to include the realm of spirits in that category.[6] But the album's frontispiece bears the words 'Heartsease' in script, and below, 'illustrated by Helios', as if the photographer of the fanciful pictures in this album wished to distance himself from the 'Muybridge' who had just completed the scientific analysis of equine locomotion.

By this time, Muybridge had gone public with the zoopraxiscope. On 4 May, following a press preview, he gave the first public demonstrations in the rooms of the Art Association. The newspapers all carried glowing accounts the next day. The *Daily Alta* celebrated the projections as laying 'the foundation of a new method of entertaining the people . . . and we predict that [Muybridge's] instantaneous, photographic, magic-lantern zoetrope will make the rounds of the civilized world'. The *San Francisco News Letter* described the images as having been 'indicated by the camera and made by the retoucher', while the *Call* emphasized their realism: 'Nothing was wanting but the clatter of hoofs upon the turf and an occasional breath of steam from the nostrils, to make the spectator believe that he had before him genuine flesh-and-blood steeds.'

In these early exhibitions, Muybridge used the projections to entertain, to prove the accuracy of his photographs and to educate. To illustrate how a short camera exposure freezes motion, for example, he used a technique first recorded in 1851 by the inventor of photography on paper, William Henry Fox Talbot, who fastened a piece of the London *Times* to a spinning disc and, darkening the room, opened his camera and discharged a spark from a Leyden jar. Like a modern-day strobe light, the spark illuminated the rotating disc for a split second to make an image as sharp as if the disc had been motionless. Repeating the experiment, Muybridge shuttered off his lantern's light as he projected a spinning spoked wheel; then, for an instant, he opened it again: 'A flash of light, imitating an electric discharge, showed the shadow, and for an instant it appeared as though the wheel had stopped.'[7]

During this experimental period, Muybridge also managed to put the finishing touches to a book. The four prototypes of *The Attitudes of Animals in Motion: A Series of Photographs Illustrating the Consecutive Positions Assumed by Animals in Performing Various Movements, Executed at Palo Alto, California, in 1878 and 1879,* each containing between 174 and 203 images, were copyrighted on 17 May 1881. A copy dedicated 15 May was inscribed to Stanford, and the date suggests that Muybridge wanted to protect himself from any other claims, including Stanford's own, to the work. Stanford's album comprised tipped-in albumen prints, a preface written by Muybridge and an index to the illustrations. Of three other prototypes, one in the Library of Congress and two others in the Kingston Museum, only the first contains the index and preface. Other final, perhaps, versions – there are fewer than ten in existence – consist of brown-toned cyanotypes or Van Dyke prints, a cheaper and speedier method for producing multiple volumes. Judging from his inscriptions, Muybridge seems to have given most of them away as presentation copies.

The first images in *Attitudes of Animals in Motion* are bird's-eye views of the Palo Alto ranch, followed by pictures of the general layout: the track and camera shed. Different cloud formations feature in these establishing views, signalling Muybridge's mastery of the medium as well as heralding the experiments that would follow. As in his previous work, Muybridge moves his camera from the general to the specific. Close-ups of the equipment itself – the cameras and their shutters – are followed by the subjects of the pictures: the horses, domestic animals and athletes. Many of these images are retouched; he outlines the silhouettes in some and 'fades out' the jockeys in others, often eliminating the backgrounds.

The pictures in *Attitudes* are organized according to the movement depicted. In his *Index to Illustrations*, he gives the 'length of stride' of each movement with notations to indicate whether the distance 'intervening between each position' was 21 or 27 inches (53.3 or 68.6 cm), or 'exposure made by means of clockwork at regulated intervals of time instead of distance'. 'Unless otherwise mentioned', he notes, 'each successive photograph illustrates the position assumed by a forward motion of 12 inches'. The horses are indexed by movement, the animals by species and movement. The athletes' pictures – also indexed by movement – begin with the simplest, walking and running, again with the length of stride noted, followed by the more complicated somersaults, 'flip flap' boxing, fencing, 'posturing' – these are pictures of poses – and a category of movement designated 'irregular'. Muybridge directs the athletes to assume the familiar positions of classical sculpture, and his treatment of them marks the beginning of a new direction where art and science will become joint subjects for his battery of cameras.

The last group of pictures in *Attitudes* consists of nine photographs of a horse's skeleton posed in different positions. Stanford's friend Dr J.D.B. Stillman had provided the skeleton. Stillman, a physician, was working with Stanford on a book about the horse that was intended for a commercial market. Under the assumption that his role in that project would be duly recognized, Muybridge seems to have collaborated with Stillman in late 1880, to the extent of writing a lengthy introduction for the proposed book. He also used the photographs of the skeleton on his zoopraxiscope disc – the only photographic material found on the discs. The supposed collaboration, however, would come back to haunt Muybridge two years later and would lead to yet another one of his lawsuits.

The Stanford family had set sail on 21 May 1880 for a summer in Europe, bringing along prints of Muybridge's experiments. While in Europe, Stanford wanted to have portraits painted: Jane Stanford's by Léon Bonnat, and his own by Jean-Louis-Ernest Meissonier. According to Meissonier's memoirs and other accounts, including his biographer's, the realist painter, who prided himself on his accurate depictions of the horses in his battle scenes, at first refused the commission until Stanford challenged him to sketch two sequential positions of a horse trotting. When Meissonier failed after three attempts, Stanford pulled out the Muybridge photographs. 'I was dumbfounded', Meissonier explained. I was no longer in business with an American millionaire. Here was something I could build on. I promised him his portrait.'[8]

Meissonier had made the study of the horse's movements his life's work, even building a miniature railroad to travel alongside of the horse in order to observe its paces. 'After thirty years of absorbing and concentrated study, I find I have been wrong', he is reported to have said. 'Never again shall I touch a brush.'[9]

Whether the dramatic story is apocryphal or not – it is difficult to believe Meissonier could have missed the publication of Muybridge's photographs in *La Nature* in December 1878 – Meissonier completed a portrait of Stanford the following year, in 1881. Now in the collection of the Iris & B. Gerald Cantor Center for Visual Arts, Stanford University, the portrait includes Muybridge's *Attitudes,* which Stanford had brought with him on his return trip to Paris in late June of that year. Meissonier depicts Stanford as he wished to be viewed: as the disinterested scientist, seated in front of a desk covered with papers and books. Below Stanford's left elbow, which rests on his favourite ivory-handled cane, one can glimpse a corner of Muybridge's volume.

Sponsored by Stanford, supposedly at the urging of Meissonier, Muybridge, too, had left San Francisco for Europe that June, stopping in New York while Stanford sailed on to London.[10] At the end of May, before the two men left the West Coast, they met to officially bring the Palo Alto experiments to a close: Stanford paid Muybridge $2,000 for his work and, in exchange for $1, relinquished 'all right to title or claim' to 'any and all photographic apparatus, consisting of cameras, lenses, electric shutters, negatives, positives and photographs, magic lanterns, zoopraxiscopes; and patents and copyrights that have been employed in, and about the representation of animals in motion upon my premises at Palo Alto.'[11]

Muybridge closed the door on his career as a landscape photographer at the same time. In the *Photographic Times and American Photographer* he advertised the sale of the Dallmeyer lenses he had used to make his beautiful views of Yosemite, his panoramas, and his pictures of San Francisco, a city he would never again make his home.

Muybridge sailed for Europe weighted down with his zoopraxiscope, glass discs, shutters and copies of *Attitudes*. After a short visit to London and probably to his Kingston relatives, whom he had not seen for almost fifteen years, Muybridge arrived in Paris. His first demonstration took place on 26 September at Étienne-Jules Marey's house on the boulevard Delessert, in the fashionable Passy district of Paris's sixteenth arrondissement. Marey had invited a large group of scientific luminaries, many of whom had come to Paris to attend the Electricity Congress. The soirée was described in the Paris *Globe*, whose editor's wife, Marie-Antoinette Elvire Vilbort, was Marey's mistress and the mother of his daughter:

> M. Marey, Professor of the College of France, yesterday invited to his new house in the Trocadero, Boulevard Delessert, some foreign and French savants, together with his intimate friend, our director, M. Vilbort. The attraction for the evening consisted of the curious experiments of Mr Muybridge, an American, in photographing the movements of animated beings.
>
> Among those invited by M. Marey were M. Helmholtz, whose name ranks high among all sciences; M. Govi, Professor of the University of Naples; M. Bjerknes, a Norwegian, whose great discoveries with respect to the laws of electricity have secured

him a place in that Congress; Messieurs Brown-Sequard, Mascart, Ango, d'Arsonval, Terquem, Lippmann, of the College of France and of the Sorbonne, Th. Villard, Municipal Counsellor; Adml. Coste, Col. Duhousset, Capt. Bonnat, Capt. Raabe, Burdeau, Professor at the Lycée of Louis the Great; Goubaux of the Alfort School; Salathé, Nadar, Gaston Tissandier, Heim, Editor in Chief of the Strasbourg Press (which M. de Manteuffel has just suppressed); etc. . . .

Mr Muybridge, an American savant, gives us the first experience of something that should be accorded to the whole Parisian public. He projects upon a white curtain photographs showing horses and other animals going at their most rapid gaits. But that is not all. His photography having taken 'on the wing' each movement of which each gait is composed, shows us the animal in the positions that our eye, taking in only the general ensemble, would not otherwise observe. M. Marey lent his cooperation to Mr Muybridge and made witty remarks on each tableau.

There was first laid before us, in this manner, the marvelous apparatus employed by Mr Muybridge. He then showed us the apparatus in position disposed to the number of 24 in a sort of stand. Each seizes upon the image of an animal as it appears before it in an instant – two hundredths of a second. Before this arrangement of apparatus ranged along like cannons, 24 in number, the animal passes along on a track, beyond which is a white wall which furnishes an appropriate background for the photography. At each step, the animal breaks a thread, which brings an instrument into play, so that at each stage of its passage no matter how rapid, there remains to us an exact image . . .

Now what conclusion is to be drawn from these curious experiments? First, they give us more intelligent instruction with respect to the movements of animals, and then permit the formulation of laws therefrom; consequently, our artists can gain from the study of this photography, more faithful than the sketches of a master of the art, valuable hints for their work. They will become accustomed, as M. Marey says, to paint after Nature, like the Japanese (in regard to birds), and to thus instruct the public.

The sitting was prolonged until late, but we regretted that the time had come, when it did, to bid adieu to M. Marey and Madame Vilbort, who did the honors of the evening so charmingly.[12]

Soon after, Marey invited Muybridge to see the beginnings of the large outdoor laboratory he was building with city funds in the Bois de Boulogne on the outskirts of the city – today the site of the Roland Garros tennis stadium, home of the French Open. Muybridge presented Marey with an inscribed copy of *Attitudes*.

Two months later, on 26 November, there was a second 'entertainment' for Muybridge, this one given at the home of Meissonier for an audience composed of 'the most famous and influential painters and critics of the official art establishment of the day'.[13] Muybridge's projectionist that evening was the lantern maker Alfred Molteni, who in 1895 would make the lamp houses for the cinématographes projectors of the Lumière brothers.

Muybridge's photographs and his zoopraxiscope lecture once again caused a sensation. Meissonier, who had been dumbfounded by the photographs when Stanford had brought them the year before had by now resigned himself to their truth. He not only based his paintings of horses on them, but also had gone back to correct earlier pictures in which the positions of the horses did not comply with what the camera showed.

Considering that Muybridge saw himself, and always referred to himself, as an artist, he would have been more at home in Meissonier's circle than in Marey's. The success he met among the artists at Meissonier's certainly would have made him feel he was one of them. As he expressed in a letter to Frank Shay, written two days after the reception, 'Happily I have strong nerves, or I should have blushed with the lavishness of [the] praises.'[14]

In Paris Muybridge finally triumphed in his role as a lecturer and an entertainer. He found himself in the midst of the most sophisticated, urbane company he could have imagined. He was applauded and feted, not as an employee of Stanford's, but for his own original contributions to the progress of art and, at least initially, of science.

Soon enough, however, Marey and other scientists found Muybridge's photographs inadequate to their needs. The photographs of birds that Muybridge had made at Marey's behest disappointed him. Muybridge had brought instantaneous images of groups of birds (these were not part of *Attitudes of Animals in Motion*), rather than images which showed the trajectory of the wing. 'Apart from the fact that the sharpness of the images was insufficient,' wrote Marey, who would overcome the inadequacies of Muybridge's system with his development of chronophotography, 'the photographs were missing the one thing that made the pictures of the gait of the horse so interesting, a series which showed the successive positions of the animal.'[15] Marey – followed by other scientists – felt that Muybridge's battery-of-cameras method was prone to inaccuracy. His subjects were not photographed from a constant perspective or from a single point of view, and the intermediary phases of the movement were too hard to assemble from the ones that were pictured. Muybridge couldn't represent the trajectory of the movement. He 'could not avoid errors that inverted the phases of the movement and brought to the eyes and spirit of those who consulted these beautiful plates a deplorable confusion.'[16]

Muybridge continued to lecture in Paris that winter. A demonstration in December for the Cercle de L'Union Artistique was greeted with the same enthusiastic ovation as that given by Meissonier's 200 guests. To capitalize on his burgeoning celebrity status, Muybridge began to seek financial support for a new and larger photographic project on animal locomotion, an ambitious endeavour that would sustain his career and guarantee ongoing acclaim within the circles he now frequented. Without outside support and collaboration, however, he could not undertake a truly scientific investigation: he simply did not have the background, training, instruments or knowledge. Muybridge knew this, and soon his scientific friends knew it as well: after the novelty of his demonstrations wore off, scientific interest in his work began to wane.

Artists, on the other hand, never lost interest in what his cameras could reveal. But Muybridge was at an impasse until he could find a patron to fund a new project that would be perceived as having some artistic, scientific or practical value. Unlike Marey, he was not aligned with a scientific institution supported by government grants or laboratory subsidies, and he was unable to provide the degree of scientific foundation that would attract outside agencies to the project. Neither the income from continued sales of his photographs nor the proceeds of his zoopraxiscope lectures were enough to subsidize a new venture. Stanford could no longer be depended on. Although he had paid for Muybridge's trip to Europe, Stanford had accomplished what he set out to do: he was now focused on the book with Stillman, which he thought would make his work internationally known.

The quest for a new backer became Muybridge's primary objective for the rest of his European sojourn. In the same November letter to Frank Shay, Muybridge informed him that he would shortly visit England 'for the purpose of inducing some wealthy gentleman (to whom I have letters of introduction) to provide the necessary funds for pursuing and indeed completing the investigations of animal motion'. And then, in a letter written on 23 December, he revealed to Shay a potentially perfect solution: a collaboration with Meissonier, Marey, and a 'capitalist' friend of Meissonier's – Muybridge didn't know his name – who would finance the project. The idea, which according to Muybridge was Meissonier's, was to publish a book illustrated by photographs that Muybridge would make 'upon the attitudes of animals in motion as illustrated by both ancient and modern artists. [Meissonier] proposes it shall be a most elaborate work, and exhaustive of the subject . . . a standard work of art which as Meissonier says will hand the names of all four of us down to posterity.'[17]

In an odd reference at the end of this letter, Muybridge makes the following invitation: 'if in the course of your travels you should next summer find yourself in Paris, make me a visit to my Electro-Photo studio in the Bois de Boulogne and I will give you a welcome.' The 'studio', although Shay would not have known this, could only have been Marey's Physiological Station, which in December was still in the preparation stages. The invitation was a bluff, an example of Muybridge's flair for self-promotion and publicity. Another bluff was Marey's supposed collaboration. The first time Marey would hear about it was in a letter Muybridge wrote to him one month after he had written to Shay:

I think it highly probable the hope you kindly express in refer-ence to the future experiments, are in a fair way of realization. M. Meissonier has ever since my acquaintance with him, taken the warmest interest in my illustrations of the attitudes of animals in motion, and has undertaken to see the means are provided for executing a new series of experiments during the coming season which I trust will completely eclipse those hitherto made, and I trust you will approve of the engagement I made him on your behalf, that we should have the advantage of your invaluable advice and assistance in the work.[18]

It was too late in any case: stirred into action by Muybridge's visit and by the commercial introduction of the fast and easy to use dry plate, Marey had begun his own photographic investigations of motion.

A month later, in February 1882, Muybridge left for London to lecture at the Royal Institution, an establishment devoted to scientific research and education, with historical ties to the birth of photography. Its first director was Sir Humphry Davy, one of the earliest experimenters with, and disseminators of, photographic processes. It was in the laboratory of its second director, Michael Faraday, a discoverer of electromagnetism, that Fox Talbot had carried out his spark photography experiments. And it was at the Royal Institution that Faraday had initiated the public scientific lecture illustrated with his own scientific experiments. Faraday's had been the most famous lectures of the nineteenth century, and now Muybridge was following in his footsteps.

On 13 March Muybridge presented his pictures of galloping horses, trotting deer and trundling pigs at the Institution to an enthralled audience of notables and dignitaries, including the Prince and Princess of Wales and their daughters, the painter Frederic Leighton, the scientist Alfred Huxley and the Poet Laureate Alfred Tennyson. Again, it was an unmitigated success. 'This pleasing display was the essence of life and reality', wrote an observer for the *Photographic News*. '[A] new world of sights and wonders was, indeed, opened by photography, which was not less astounding because it was truth itself.'[19] The writer went on to describe the following exchange:

'I should like to see your boxing pictures', said the Prince of Wales to Mr Muybridge . . . 'I shall be very happy to show them, your Royal Highness', responded the clever photographer; and promptly there was thrown upon the screen two athletes who pounded away at each other right merrily, to the infinite delight of the audience in general and the Prince of Wales in particular . . . 'I don't know that these pictures teach us anything very useful', said Mr Muybridge, 'but they are generally found amusing'.[20]

Both photographic journals and the popular press reported Muybridge's Royal Institution lectures and those he gave over the following days at the Royal Academy of Arts and the Savage Club. In April he lectured at Eton College, near Windsor, and then back in London at the science and art department of the South Kensington Museum, a building exactly across the street from the site of the 1862 Great London Exposition, where Muybridge had exhibited his washing machine and printing plate apparatus twenty years earlier. Now he had returned home in triumph. And it was here, as he carved out a new renown for himself in his homeland, that he altered his name for the last time. Adopting the medieval spelling of the Saxon kings who had been crowned in Kingston, Edward became Eadweard.[21]

The California papers gave news of his success abroad. 'In all my long experience of London life I cannot recall a single instance where such warm tributes of admiration for merit have been unstintingly given by the greatest of the land', wrote the London correspondent of the San Francisco *Call*.[22] But the applause was abruptly silenced by an embarrassing incident that brought Muybridge's 'promising career in London . . . to a disastrous close'.[23] On 20 April the London science journal *Nature* noted the appearance of the book Stillman and Stanford had collaborated on. *The Horse in Motion as Shown by Instantaneous Photography, with a Study on Animal Mechanics, Founded on Anatomy and the Revelations of the Camera, in Which is Demonstrated the Theory of Quadrupedal Locomotion* was 'executed and published under the auspices of Leland Stanford'. Five of Muybridge's photographs and 91 lithographs made from the rest of the pictures he had taken in California appeared in *The Horse in Motion*, but Muybridge was not credited anywhere on the title page. Stanford had relegated him to the role of technician only. Worse, Stillman had rejected the lengthy introduction which Muybridge had believed would be his contribution to the collaboration.

As a result, the Royal Society, which had invited Muybridge to submit a paper on animal locomotion to be published in their *Proceedings* – and, according to Muybridge, had promised to provide the funds for an exhaustive investigation of the subject to be made under their auspices – no longer welcomed him. Under the direction of referee Francis Galton, a cousin of Charles Darwin and a photographer in his own right, the committee rejected the paper: compared to Stillman's, the committee judged Muybridge's account to be poorly written; he was seen as having misrepresented his role in the 'chronophotographic work, and to have been merely an opportunistic employee of Stanford'.[24] The blow to his pride can only be imagined.

But he had not abandoned hope of restoring his reputation in Europe. Just before sailing for New York, Muybridge wrote to Marey with an urgent appeal to rekindle the possibilities of a collaboration:

During your absence in Italy M. Meissonier became very much interested in my photographs of animal movements and expressed his willingness to associate himself with me, or with you and me, in the production of an elaborate work on the subject of the results of my investigations. However, M. Meissonier finds it difficult to decide, or to act promptly. I have delayed publishing the photographs excepting in the form of the large volumes of which I have sold a few for $100, or £21, and if I can make any arrangement with you alone, or with you and M. Meissonier, I will delay publishing in the other manner. I am satisfied a book containing a good selection of subjects, an edition de luxe, at a price of about 100 francs, will have a very large sale.

I am willing to enter into any equitable arrangement with you and if you wish will give you the exclusive right to use the subjects you select for illustration, on the continent, and will accept in return the exclusive right to your text for England and America . . .

If you cannot secure the aid of M. Meissonier I am perfectly willing to make an arrangement with you alone.[25]

On 5 June Muybridge set sail for America, where he launched a lawsuit against both Stanford and the publisher of *The Horse in Motion*, J. R. Osgoode & Co., for copyright infringement.

In July, Muybridge wrote once more to Marey, this time introducing 'Heartsease' owner Robert C. Johnson, who was 'interested enough in the subject of animal mechanism to try and find money' for a collaborative project:

> It was my hope that M. Johnson would have arranged to induce both yourself and M. Meissonier to contribute to the publication of a book much upon the scale I projected and which M. Meissonier approved would perhaps have cost 75 to 100,000 francs to get up. He was willing to enter into this, not only from his desire to contribute to science but also from his friendship for me and his wish to thwart the contemptible tricks of a man whom I thought was a generous friend, but whose liberality turns out to have been an instrument for his own glorification . . .
>
> Now whether Robert C. Johnson joins me or not I am now resolved to publish the results of my investigations. I should have preferred for you to have joined in the preparation of an elaborate and comprehensive work. If that cannot be I will publish the photographic results alone and without any analysis.
>
> M. Meissonier has very kindly offered to write a preface to the book, on the association of the results with art and their possible relation and influence with art; and if your numerous and important occupations will permit may I beg the favour of your writing me an introduction from a scientific point of view. If you will do this I shall not fail in my endeavours to reciprocate by all means in my power.

I have made arrangements to give a course of public lectures illustrated with [the] Zoopraxiscope, in the various cities of the United States, commencing in August, and if you will permit me to announce my intended publication with an introduction by you it will aid me very much and I shall be much gratified by the receipt of such manuscript as you may feel inclined to write as early as the value of your time will permit.[26]

The collaboration did not materialize. And in 1885 Muybridge lost both lawsuits. He would never forget Stanford's betrayal. In the last paragraph of his *Animal Locomotion*, entitled 'Retrospective', Muybridge reminded the reader that 'a number of his early experimental photographs of animal movements, and his original Title . . . were copied, and published a few years ago.'

Back in America, Stillman's publication did little harm to Muybridge's reputation. He actually enjoyed great success with the public lectures he mentioned to Marey, demonstrating his zoopraxiscope in Newport, Boston and New York. His lecture now primarily promoted photography as a scientific instrument with which to correct the errors of artists. In February 1883 he projected his images in Philadelphia at The Franklin Institute and at the Pennsylvania Academy of the Fine Arts. By March he had already produced a preliminary prospectus for a 'new and elaborate work upon the attitudes of man, the horse and other animals in motion', in which we can see the kernel of what would become *Animal Locomotion* with its fusion of popular entertainment, aesthetics and science. The new work was to include 'photographs of actors performing their respective parts, works of art from the Museums, Picture Galleries and Libraries of Europe', photographs of 'trajectory curves' that he would make with Marey's 'photographic revolver', and an essay by Marey himself. If that were not enough, the subscriber could 'send a horse or other animal or subject to my studio for a special photographic analysis of its movements which will be illustrated without extra charge'.[27] Muybridge promised the photographs to be positive prints made from negatives, not lithographic reproductions, which he pointed out were absolutely worthless for scientific or artistic use – an obvious jab at the Stillman book, which was illustrated primarily by lithographs.

It was the lecture at the Pennsylvania Academy of the Fine Arts that helped Muybridge find his new patron. There he met Thomas Eakins, the painter who had written to him about his photographs in 1878, and the Academy's then head Fairman Rogers, with whom he had also been in correspondence. Seconded by Eakins, Rogers persuaded William Pepper, provost of the University of Pennsylvania, to fund a new photographic study. In August 1883 the university issued an invitation to Muybridge to continue his work under their auspices. A group of wealthy and interested Philadelphians, including Coleman Sellers, guaranteed an initial outlay of $5,000 for the project and Muybridge began work at his new base the following summer.

8

Making *Animal Locomotion*

Muybridge began photographing at the University of Pennsylvania in June 1884. Pepper had assigned him four assistants, and had put a patch of land at his disposal, between the two wings of the newly created Veterinary Department, where a 120-foot (36.6 m) fenced-out track was laid. Pepper also put together a commission to oversee the work: 'It was represented to the Trustees of the University that several individuals appreciating the importance of the proposed work to art and science would unite in guaranteeing all expenses connected with the investigation if a University Commission would be appointed to supervise the entire affair and thus insure its thoroughly scientific character.'[1] This was an unusual procedure; it might have been necessary because the project would be using naked human beings as subjects, which raised inevitable concerns – Eakins, for example, would be fired from the Academy of the Fine Arts in 1886 for undraping a male model in a mixed class.

The committee of nine professors and doctors included Eakins, neurologist Francis X. Dercum, anatomist Joseph Leidy, physiologist Harrison Allen and engineer William Marks. Each man intended to have Muybridge photograph particular subjects, but all were united in the belief that the camera could be used as an aid to science. The committee must have had confidence in Muybridge's capacity as a sophisticated and innovative photographer: they met only once and rarely came to watch what he was doing. Muybridge appreciated the status the committee provided – it gave his work, he claimed, 'additional weight and value', as he was 'neither a physiologist nor an anatomist' – but his appreciation would not in any way stifle his own creative impulses.[2] With *Animal Locomotion*, Muybridge would serve two masters: his scientific committee and his artistic vocation. The association with a famous university and a group of reputable scientists was something Muybridge had sought since he left London in 1882. He was willing to do their bidding, and would carry out the work with his usual commitment and concentration, but at the same time he would realize his own goals. The university's attempt to ensure the scientific integrity of the project would be only partially successful, but Muybridge's own ambitions would come to full fruition.

Eakins was with Muybridge when he began to photograph on the grounds of the University. An accomplished photographer in his own right, Eakins had photographed his family and friends as models for his paintings, and he also used the camera in his

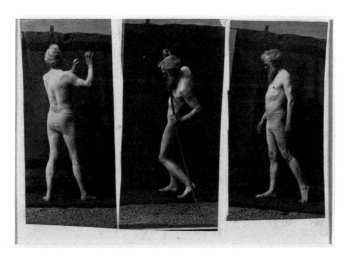

Muybridge posing, 1884; the photograph was probably taken by Thomas Eakins or Thomas Anschutz.

classes at the Pennsylvania Academy of the Fine Arts. Either Eakins, or his student Thomas Anschutz who was also present, took a set of three pictures of Muybridge posing. Dressed only in a pair of white shorts, he stands against a black backdrop in profile with his back to the camera. In one image, he leans on a pole as if punting on a river and, in another, looks up and gesticulates with his hands as if contemplating an apparition. The third shows him gazing down, his left leg extended behind him. These gestures, emulating classical sculptures, were amongst the first images made that June.

Eakins and Muybridge used the dry plate, not the collodion wet plate with which Muybridge had made his reputation. The dry plate was much faster: it also was a completely industrialized and standardized product. Dry plates – the sensitive silver was held in a dry gelatin emulsion – were made in factories and typically sold in boxes of a dozen; each plate was already precoated ready to be put in a camera and exposed.

Eakins and Muybridge also experimented with different cameras, the first being one that functioned like a zoopraxiscope in reverse. Here is how Thomas Anschutz described the initial stages of the work:

> Maybridge [*sic*] as you know is carrying on his scheme over at the University. He has a small enclosure . . . also a machine for taking views on one plate, of moving objects, by opening and closing the camera rapidly at the rate of about 100 exposures per second. This shows the moving object not as a continuous smeer [*sic*] but shows one clear view at every 2 or 3 inches of advance. The exposures are made by two large discs with openings cut around their circumferences. They run in opposite directions and are geared to run very fast, the exposure is while the two openings meet. The lens remains uncapped until the object has reached the edge of the plate.

Eakins, Godley and I were out there yesterday trying a machine. Eakins had made one of the above design except he had only one wheel. We sewed some bright balls on Godley and ran him down the track. The result was not very good although you could see the position of the buttons at every part of the step.

But afterwards Muybridge took him with his machine and got a very good result even showing his black clothes.

Eakins is on the committee which superintends Muybridge. He is of course much interested in the experiments. Muybridge has not made very rapid progress and the University people seem to be losing faith in him. But he showed a good result yesterday on the machine.[3]

Because his plates were subject to fogging, Eakins soon switched to a variation of the Marey-wheel camera – a single camera with a single lens that remains open while a rotating slotted-disk shutter alternately exposes and masks the plate behind it. He felt that the Marey-wheel camera provided a more accurate and useful rendering of time and space in the photographs. Muybridge seems to have made some pictures with such an apparatus, though none remain; by August, according to Anschutz, Muybridge still hadn't made much progress in any direction. The University, which had hired him to make serial photography, was not pleased:

[Muybridge] is making some very nice photographs of men and women doing things. Such as throwing, jumping stepping down and up etc. These are all made as I crudely explained on one plate. So that it shows the figure at intervals of a few inches as it goes through the movement. These images, of course frequently overlap but do not seem to confuse on that account. This work is, of course, done with one lense [*sic*]. He has not yet done any work with his series of lenses and I hear they do not work. The shutters are too clumsy and slow. The university people are dissatisfied with the affair as he cannot give them the result they expected. Which was to photograph the walk of diseased people paralytics etcr. so that by means of the zoopraxiscope (help!!!) they could show their peculiarities to the medical student. This it seems however cannot be done even with the best known contrivances. So they would like to fire the whole concern but they have gone too far to back out.[4]

Muybridge moved forward with his usual single-mindedness. He didn't seem very interested in following Eakins's suggestions to use the Marey-wheel camera; Muybridge was, after all, the more accomplished – and acclaimed – photographer and not one to follow in anyone else's footsteps. Perhaps the sheer pleasure of setting up and handling his complicated arrangement of cameras and shutters thrilled him more than operating the single camera. Whatever the reason, Eakins soon became disenchanted with Muybridge, 'whose showmanship was so at odds with [Eakins's] own public reticence',[5] and went off to photograph at a studio he had set up behind his house.

Without Eakins and while all of the rest of the committee except Dr Dercum was on vacation, Muybridge worked on his own that summer. He continued photographing from May to October 1885, and, beginning in November, he and his assistants started to compile the more than 20,000 negatives that would be assembled into a final selection of 781 plates. Originally, the publication was to be supervised by J. B. Lippincott, whose outlay of $5,000 had made it possible for Muybridge to buy new lenses in London (these were later sold to reimburse Lippincott). In the end, given the scope of the project – Muybridge's proposal to make large collotype plates measuring $19\frac{1}{8} \times 24\frac{3}{8}$ inches (48.6 × 61.9 cm), and the overall cost (close to $30,000) – the plates were published by the New York Photogravure Company, which was given the rights to the *Prospectus and Catalogue of Plates*, the marketing tool Muybridge published in 1887. By January potential subscribers could look at specimen plates in Philadelphia in January 1887, and by October proofs were available for viewing in New York, in Washington at the Corcoran Gallery and in Boston. Muybridge was given sole credit for the work, published under his name as *Animal Locomotion: An Electro-Photographic Investigation of Consecutive Phases of Animal Movements*.[6]

Organized into eleven volumes, the 781 plates that make up *Animal Locomotion* seem just what a scientific atlas of movement in the late nineteenth century should be. They are organized according to movement – as were *Attitudes* – and then by costume, with the nude coming first followed by categories of semi-draped and clothed. But there is also a hierarchy embedded in the organization of the plates in *Animal Locomotion* that is missing in the smaller *Attitudes*.

The first four volumes of plates in *Animal Locomotion* are devoted to the nude, and the first subjects are men: walking, running, jumping and then performing actions with props. Photographs of the movements of women follow those of men; children, the disabled and finally domestic and wild animals appear in turn. The very last image, Plate 781, is *Chickens Frightened by a Torpedo*. The scientific 'logic', in other words, follows a covert sociological hierarchy, from the movements of the highest subject 'the nude male' to the lowest, animals. It also moves from the more visually intelligible to the more obscure: the most difficult pictures, in which the movement is hardest to determine, are placed towards the end of each volume, where they are less noticeable. Finally, each plate bears a number corresponding to a description of the action as published by Muybridge in the accompanying *Prospectus and Catalogue of Plates.* Some titles, for example, Plate 279: *Base-ball; Batting*, seem almost superfluous. Others such as Plate 176: *Crossing Brook on Step-stones, with Fishing-pole and Basket* and Plate 270: *Arising from the Ground with Pamphlet in Left Hand* direct the viewer to imagine a narrative context for the actions.

But the published organization of *Animal Locomotion* is not the order in which Muybridge made the images. The first photographs, made in June 1884, were not of a man walking, but rather of a Mrs Cooper, holding hands with a child, carrying him, and in a second group of pictures, spanking him, or pretending to. Mrs Cooper was an artist's model, a widow 'aged 35, somewhat slender and above the medium height'.[7] She and most of the female models we see in *Animal Locomotion* had been introduced to Muybridge by J. Liberty Tadd, director of the Industrial School of Art. It seems natural that as an artist and a friend of Eakins, Muybridge would have made the acquaintance of other artists in Philadelphia. Although we have no record of how Muybridge met Tadd, the photographer used models Tadd had chosen and photographed Tadd himself (in close-ups, including his hands drawing a circle and tapping a rhythm) as well as his wife and daughter, Edith, who appears in more than fifteen plates of *Animal Locomotion*.

When Muybridge photographed Mrs Cooper and the child, he used five or six cameras placed in a semicircle around them; the shutters triggered simultaneously. The resulting 'tracking shots' showed a single gesture frozen in time from five or six different points of view, as if the viewer were walking around the posed model, although when read vertically the images of spanking suggest a chronological sequence. Why Muybridge reverted to the format he had used so effectively at the end of his work for Stanford at Palo Alto is not known. Perhaps it was taking longer than he had expected to adapt his cameras and shutters to the new dry-plate process, or perhaps he had in mind a new way of capturing movement. Whatever the reason, he made almost 100 of these tracking shots. And since they are the first images he made for *Animal Locomotion*, they are important indicators of exactly what he intended his role to be in this massive project.

Muybridge photographed his models before the same black backdrop he had posed in front of. There was no grid marking off this space as there would be in the later sequences and rather than parsing or analysing the model's movement, these early pictures clarify what Muybridge had always emphasized in his photographs: the spectacular nature of what a camera, in the hands of a virtuoso photographer, could do. And now, with the new dry plate, he could do even more. These first pictures announce one of his goals for this new body of work: to show that single isolated moment a camera alone can capture, that instant in which the laws of gravity no longer seem to prevail.

In these images, in embryonic form, are all the aesthetic motifs that would reappear obsessively throughout *Animal Locomotion*. In addition to the body suspended in mid-air, he presents us with the frozen arc of water thrown from a bucket or bowl, the fluttering of women's dresses, the twirling of a parasol. We find again the poses or movements with vases, jugs, baskets and other props that emulate those in the paintings and sculptures that had been his inspiration since leaving England as a young man. Of unlikely interest to scientists or doctors, these are the motifs, poses, gestures and artistic references to which Muybridge would return whenever he was safe from the eyes and interference of his commissioners.

Muybridge, who at 54 describes himself in the *Prospectus and Catalogue of Plates* as an 'ex-athlete, aged about sixty', appears more than once in these earliest pictures. We don't know who tripped the shutters, but he is depicted in the act of walking, climbing a ladder, throwing a disk, swinging a pickaxe, digging, sawing and hammering, using a hatchet, sitting down, sprinkling water and drinking. His naked body is lean and sinewy, his hair and beard long and white. Muybridge's rather dishevelled look did not go unnoticed by Dr Dercum: 'He was so busy that he did not have much time to go to a barber and therefore his hair and beard were at times unduly long';[8] his clothes, too, apparently left something to be desired: provost Pepper remarked on a hole in Muybridge's hat and told him that now that he was associated with the University,

Mrs Cooper 'Spanking a child', Plate 527, *Animal Locomotion*, 1887, collotype.

Muybridge 'Using pick' from Plate 52, *Animal Locomotion*, 1887, collotype.

he needed to dress better.[9] But Pepper's words had no effect. Muybridge was obsessed by his work and the opportunities it had opened to him; his personal appearance was the last thing on his mind.

By August 1884 Muybridge was operating with a battery of twelve cameras on three subjects: the university athletes, Dr Dercum's disabled patients and Mrs Cooper, dressed and undressed. In these, the first sequences of photographs, narrow wooden boards marked off at intervals were fixed to the near and far edges of the track to allow for the measurement of the space being traversed. At the end of the month, he took the cameras to the Philadelphia Zoological Garden to photograph storks and swans in flocks, a sloth moving along a pole, a camel trotting and galloping away from the camera, a crane flapping its wings and deer leaping over one another. His cameras were not accurately synchronized, however; he did not yet have the capacity to photograph birds in flight, and most of the images, he confessed, were not publishable.

After a winter on the road with the zoopraxiscope, all the while soliciting subscriptions for his new project, Muybridge returned to his cameras in June 1885. On 2 June his subject was the 'mulatto pugilist' Ben Bailey. And in the photographs of Bailey (see overleaf), we can observe for the first time in the background a grid made up of white threads divided in two-inch (5.1 cm) squares.

That the grid makes its debut behind the only black model among the 95 who posed for Muybridge tells us a lot about the specific interests of the committee. Although artists had long used grids to ensure the accuracy of the proportions in their pictures, the grid found in *Animal Locomotion* has its origins in anthropology. It was borrowed from one devised by English ethnologist J. H. Lamprey and presented to the Ethnological Society of London in 1869. Like the one seen behind Bailey, Lamprey's grid was a 'cross-sectional mesh constructed from "threads" stretched 2 inches apart, both horizontally and vertically on a 3 x 7 ft frame'.[10] Lamprey had used the grid to assist in comparative morphological measurement in his photographs of Malay natives.

The insertion of such a grid into Muybridge's project indicates that Bailey is an object of anthropological scrutiny. In the 1870s the anthropological object was invariably the non-white body, belonging to the physically and culturally different 'other' that colonial expansion and consolidation had introduced to Europe in larger numbers than ever before. Anthropological description of these bodies was aimed at collecting comparative data in order to produce pictorial evidence of racial typologies. These descriptions, in turn, were used to support an evolutionary hierarchy of races in which whiteness was at the apex. The presumed superiority of the white man to the non-white was based upon assumptions that circulated with popularized Darwinism. The most fundamental of these was the particular definition of 'race' itself, which joined the physical, biological nature of man to his cultural, moral and intellectual nature. The emergence of scientific anthropology at this time was supported by positivist beliefs about the validity of observation, recording and classification, and photography helped transform these activities into a visible, permanent and measurable form.

Joseph Leidy, a member of the Ethnological Society of London, was likely the committee member who suggested using the grid. He and fellow members Harrison Allen, Pepper and Dercum would all be founding members in 1889 of the American Anthropometric

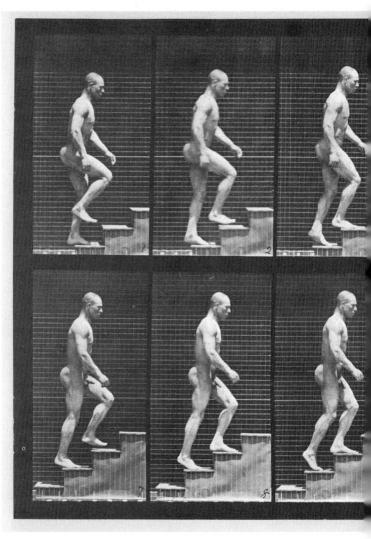

Ben Bailey 'Ascending stairs', Plate 91, *Animal Locomotion*, 1887, collotype.

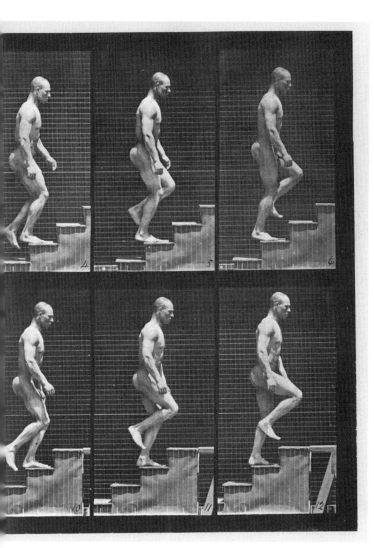

Society, devoted to a subdiscipline of anthropology that defined racial difference by the measurement of physical disparities such as skull size. For them, Bailey would have been the perfect subject. Not only was he a black man, but he was a boxer – having a body with the kind of overdeveloped musculature that defined their notion of the 'primitive'.

After Bailey's appearance, Muybridge began to photograph examples of 'civilized' masculinity – the university's student athletes – against the grid. These photographs were taken at the behest of Pepper, whose chief goal for the university was to develop a modern system of physical education and hygiene. Pepper wanted Muybridge to photograph the university's star athletes because he needed visual examples of what his methods could produce: vigorous, evenly developed bodies that would withstand neurasthenia, or 'American nervousness'. This 'disease of civilization', seen by the medical profession as resulting from the inhuman pace of modern life, was perceived as a threat to America's 'brain workers', the college-educated professionals. Since the 1870s elite American universities had attempted to reshape American sports on the English model, as a way both of establishing the social distinctiveness of the new American middle class and of separating it from the growing working class, particularly immigrants. In the minds of pioneers like Pepper, the physical prowess of the university's athletes (who were amateurs, not professional sportsmen) would be a manifest-ation of their moral superiority, representative of the values of the American way of life. To that end, Pepper had Muybridge photo-graph the athletes not just walking and running but engaged in amateur sports such as rowing, wrestling, baseball, football and cricket; these images were intended to show the beneficiaries of Pepper's system in action as well as to present them as paradigms of the specimens he hoped to develop.

For the photographs of the athletes, Muybridge expanded his batteries of cameras from one to three so that he could photograph the models from the side, back and front simultaneously. This was a completely innovative arrangement that fulfilled the needs of both science and art: anthropologists wanted the specimens photographed from the front and the side, and artists desired to have three-dimensional images from which to draw.

From this time onward, Muybridge usually used twelve cameras parallel to the model, which took what he called the 'lateral' views, and two single cameras each with a bank of twelve lenses (plus a focusing lens), shutters, and plate holders at 60 and 90 degrees to his subject, which made what he called 'foreshortened' views. He less often made up to 36 lateral views of the subject employing both the 'lateral' and 'foreshortened' cameras. The plate holders for the single cameras held three narrow sheets (about 3 inches – 7.6 cm – high) of glass, each 12 inches (30.5 cm) long, so that four images were made on each. To trigger all 36 shutters simultaneously, he devised, with the help of University of Pennsylvania engineers, an electric circuit breaker which he called his 'exposor motor'.

Throughout June 1885 Muybridge photographed more than 200 sequences, including the athletes running, playing baseball, heaving rocks and doing acrobatics; two dogs, 'Ike' and 'Maggie'; a number of horses; ponies who did tricks such as ringing bells, standing on Teeter boards, rolling boxes and jumping over each other; a mule called 'Denver' who was also trained to do tricks, including 'undressing the professor' and being bucked by a man; blacksmiths; Dr Dercum's patients; and a Mr Craig Arnold, who was photographed turning a crank handle and lying down and rising from a couch. July saw a predominance of female subjects, presumably because both the students and the professors were on vacation. In August Muybridge took his cameras to the zoo again, where he photographed birds and the caged animals. *The Evening Telegraph* described some of these sessions:

The Professor, protected from the sun by an old straw hat, walks about the field like a Western stock farmer. He fixes the slides, gives out the orders, like the mate of a schooner in a gale, and when everything is ready the Professor sits on a small beer keg, holding an electric key in his hand, and calls up the birds.

On 22 August the *Philadelphia Press* described the attempts of the 'bronzed and patriarchal' Muybridge, stroking 'his Rip Van Winkle beard thoughtfully', as he contemplated photographing George the lion in his cage. Muybridge explained to the reporter that he was at a disadvantage because the strong sunlight threw shadows of the bars of the cage onto the lion. He would 'like the chance to take one in his native jungle, about to pounce on his prey, but as that is impossible, we have to be content with what we can get'.

Back at the University in September, Muybridge again worked with Blanche Epler, who seems to have been his favourite model, and spent a day photographing Miss Coleman, who was joined in the afternoon by Mrs Mitchell in one series that has them meeting and another in which the former chases the latter with a broom. Then he went on to more serious subjects, photographing horses, bricklayers, boxers, blacksmiths, and once again the athletes – wrestling, rowing, shot-putting and pole vaulting. On 28 October, to finish up the project, he spent the day photographing J. A. Scott playing cricket. The very last image that day was the one of three chickens taking off as a firecracker landed in their midst.

Muybridge's *Prospectus and Catalogue of Plates* includes descriptive information about his subjects: the identifying number of the model (the animals were listed by species and by name, if they had one); the movement portrayed; the profession of the male models; and the marital status, weight and age of the females. He also provides technical information: the arrangement of cameras; the temporal intervals between one image and the next; and the exposure times for each. From the notes detailing possible irregularities and other caveats he appended to these measurements, however, we know that he had a number of problems with his equipment. The cameras – in particular the foreshortening shutters – often were not triggered sequentially, and some not at all; the negatives were fogged, and many of the exposure times and intervals had not been recorded. As he admitted, 'perfect uniformity of time, speed and distance was not always obtained'.

And yet the problems created by the limitations of his apparatus are not immediately apparent. This is because the individual images are published as sequences, and the way Muybridge arranged the series on the plate masks the difficulties he had. From his notebooks we know that he usually made 12 lateral and 24 foreshortened views of each subject; yet only about half of the published prints contain 36 intact images. Where a phase of movement was missing, Muybridge would assemble the negatives that remained, give them internal consistency and renumber them to appear consecutively in the print. There are even some prints whose individual elements were culled from separate picture-taking sessions. Where gaps between phases were the most blatant, the leftover pieces were still assembled and numbered consecutively and then titled 'miscellaneous'. Another creative solution he came up with for dealing with gaps in a series or an incomplete series was to make the lateral and foreshortened views congruent on the page. He could replace a missing image by enlarging one image to fill the space of two, by printing one image in the series twice, by removing the central section of an image and abutting the remaining parts or by substituting a view of the empty backdrop taken from a view-point consistent with the rest of the series. These tactics – expansion, insertion, contraction and substitution – were all useful in giving such series the cohesion and logic that Muybridge intended, even when technical difficulties interfered with his goals. That such dis-junctions have remained largely unnoticed is not all that surprising – because they are presented as sequences, we see them that way.

Blanche Epler 'Ascending and descending stairs', Plate 504, *Animal Locomotion*, 1887, collotype.

Any cues that might tip us off to the irregularities have been obliterated within the overall effect: the backgrounds are identical, the images are for the most part the same size and the series are aligned with each other and on the page.

Though Muybridge's matching of lateral and foreshortened views as well the logic of the sequential structure make the inconsistencies invisible to the casual viewer, there are in fact missing phases of movement, some accounted for in the *Prospectus* and some not. There is no movement at all in certain images, while in others purportedly chronological sequences display two different sets of consecutive numbers, one in the negative and one in the print. There are sequences in which the figures in the supposedly matching horizontal and vertical images do not match, and there are sequences that have clearly been made at different times but are pieced together to compose a single plate. Plate 504, for example, shows Blanche Epler walking up and down stairs with a bowl of water in her hands, but in the third image, a water jug has suddenly taken the place of the bowl. Two sets of numbers can be seen in some of the individual images in this sequence. Similarly, in Plate 202, the position of the handkerchief dropping from Blanche's hands is different in the third lateral and foreshortened views.

The contact proofs Muybridge made from his negatives, rediscovered in 1999 in storage in the Smithsonian Institution, shine a light on the problems that the final collotype sequences hide. These proofs are cyanotypes, photographs that, like blueprints, are made with iron rather than silver salts. They originally belonged to J. B. Colt & Co., the New York lantern-slide manufacturer, and were probably intended to be used as references for making slides from the individual negatives for sale. The cyanotypes are mounted on board and labelled with the plate number assigned to *Animal Locomotion*, a negative series number, the costume category – nude, pelvis cloth, draped – and the total number of lateral and foreshortened views that Muybridge took.

Because his negatives are lost – it is said that he buried them in the backyard of the house in Kingston he returned to in 1897 – the cyanotypes are the only remaining traces of what he originally photographed. Using the cyanotypes as his guide, Muybridge and his assistants would print each negative onto another piece of glass, assemble these positives, bind them together with tape to make a large composite, and then put the composite on a light table to print a collodion-gelatin negative. From the negative, a glass or metal plate – also lost – that had been sensitized with bichromated gelatin would be exposed, inked, and printed to make the collotypes that appear in *Animal Locomotion*.

The cyanotypes bear Muybridge's notations, the Xs or circles he used to indicate that the shutter did not fire, or had fired too soon, or that the negative had fogged and he therefore needed to compensate for it in the finished plate. And they also make clear just how much work went into making those plates. Muybridge has enlarged some negatives and cropped others to make his positives, then moved the positives around and assembled them together to make the deceptively cohesive patterns of laterals and foreshortenings we see in the final plate. The most common arrangement (a lateral series printed on one line with a rear foreshortened view beneath it and a front foreshortened view under that) is only one of 36 variations he devised. Even the plates vary in dimension and orientation to best accommodate Muybridge's editing. The cyanotypes, in short, show us that *Animal Locomotion* is a project whose every element has been subject to one kind of manipulation or another.

And in fact, in his *Prospectus and Catalogue of Plates*, Muybridge alerted viewers to certain instances in which 'it will be found that the number of phases of motion from each of the respective points of view do not correspond, some being omitted'. But the viewer, warned to expect that an image in a sequence might be missing, certainly would have been surprised to find that his or her forbearance was

Frames from cyanotype proof for Plate 504, *Animal Locomotion*, 'Ascending and descending stairs', 1885.

supposed to extend to sequences that included misaligned images made to look aligned, and plates that were composed of disparate images. What was critical for him was the appearance of congruency of the images in the print, the appearance of a logical progression and the picture's aesthetic appearance. Throughout Muybridge's work, the facts presented to his cameras and the picture of those facts he offered to the viewer often differed. He used his cameras as much to construct and deconstruct visible reality as to replicate it. Nowhere is that clearer than in *Animal Locomotion*.

The variety of the patterns of lateral and foreshortened views that Muybridge devised in order to create the appearance of congruency cannot, however, be accounted for solely in terms of his need to compensate for mechanical failures. The images also answer to the claims of art. The inspiration for the photographs that make up Plates 321 and 531 is the academic nude, and Muybridge may have intended photographs such as these specifically for artists. But because *Animal Locomotion* was funded as a scientific project, and not as a model book for artists, Muybridge has positioned the images of Blanche Epler so that she seems to rotate from one to the next. The effect is that we perceive movement, even when there is none. The negatives for the figure studies that make up Plate 201, also clearly inspired by academic painting, were taken at random intervals, but the montage made from them has a graphic force produced by a symmetrical design of contrasting patterns. In Plates 522 and 524 the arrangement of rows of tracking shots testifies to Muybridge's notion of an aesthetic effect based on symmetry and repetition. He has matched the images so that when read vertically, a sharp front-and-back rhythm occurs, while the horizontal movement gives the sensation of time being dilated as the eye slowly moves around the figure from frame to frame.

The cyanotypes are also a kind of Rosetta Stone, allowing us to decipher the notebooks Muybridge kept during the project, now housed at the George Eastman House, International Museum of

Photography and Film in Rochester, New York. In these notebooks Muybridge recorded a sequential negative series number for each session, the model's name and a description of the movement, the time spent photographing and other mechanical details. As mentioned above, the published plates are numbered and ordered in a sequence that is not related to the chronological order in which they were made. Now, because the cyanotype labels contain both the negative series number and the plate number, we can reconstitute the original order and apply each notebook description to the corresponding plate. The results are extraordinary.

Often the notebook titles differ from the plate titles published in the *Prospectus*. Plate 239: *Two models; one standing, the other sitting, crossing legs* is 'Miss N[ellie] placing chair & Miss M[amie] sitting on it' in the notebooks; Plate 73: *Turning around in surprise and running away* is 'Ashamed'. Plates 427, 428 and 429: *Toilet; two models, 1 disrobing 8* is 'Inspecting a slave (white)'. Plate 406: *Two models, 8 pouring bucket of water over 1* is 'Miss A[imer] giving miss C[ooper] a bath'. 'Relinquishing drapery for nature's garb' is the notebook shorthand for sequences of women taking off their clothes. The notebooks also attach names to the individual models identified only by number in the *Prospectus* and show that the artist's models were paid by the hour.

Many scholars have remarked on the social construction of gender in these images: how the women undertake activities not usually associated with a study of scientific locomotion and proscribed by modesty and social norms; and how the male models are depicted playing sports or engaged in professions while the women carry out domestic chores such as scrubbing and sweeping, flirt with fans, dance half-naked, or languish passively. The way in which Muybridge has recorded the models' names in the notebooks is indicative of other inequalities. Muybridge identifies some only by first name – Mamie, Nellie and Lily – and they are always photographed in the nude. 'Mrs Tadd', on the other hand, the wife of

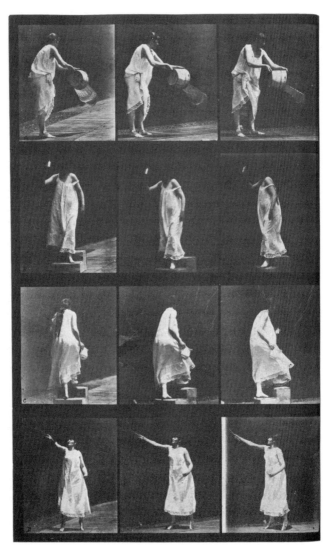

Mrs Cooper 'A: Throwing water from a bucket. B: Descending a step. C: Ascending a step. D: Playing lawn tennis', Plate 524, *Animal Locomotion*, 1887, collotype.

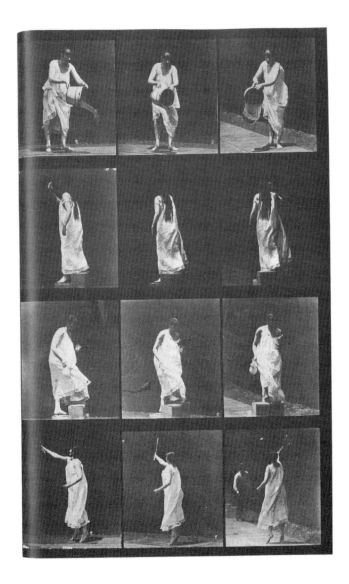

Mrs Cooper and Catherine Aimer, 'Woman disrobing another', from Plate 429, *Animal Locomotion*, 1887, collotype.

J. Liberty Tadd, is always clothed. The student athletes are recorded with their full names (and are the only ones shown posing, like Greek gods), while the professional fencers, boxers and tradesmen are known only by their last names. These latter, as Muybridge later lamented, were exceedingly modest: he had 'the greatest difficulty . . . in inducing mechanics at any price to go through the motions of their trade in a nude condition to the waist only'.[11]

Additionally, the notebooks illuminate the disparity between Muybridge's aims and those of the committee. Their academic interest in having photographs that would illustrate their concerns with health, race and class vied with Muybridge's own concern with art and narrative.

The university athletes, the boxer Ben Bailey, the professional sportsmen and tradesmen, the disabled patients, the animals at the zoo and the horses at the driving park – Muybridge photographed

all of these and other subjects in order to illustrate and demonstrate his committee's scientific concerns and hypotheses. He photographed the other models, particularly the women, with his own, primarily aesthetic, narrative concerns in mind.

Both men and women walk, run, jump, move with props and throw buckets of water, but the men are usually involved in feats of strength that make their muscles visible – they lift, carry and throw big rocks and heave logs; they pose as farmers and miners. The women carry out domestic chores – they sweep, dust, scrub floors and lift cups, glasses, bowls, jugs and vases. But they also perform particularly awkward or ungainly movements and carry out activities, like smoking, that would have been frowned upon, being associated with 'loose' women. Muybridge often photographs them in gestures we now recognize as coming from the standard pornographic vocabulary. Naked women kneel in supplication or meet and kiss, disrobe themselves and each other, dump buckets of water over each other's heads or down each other's throats.

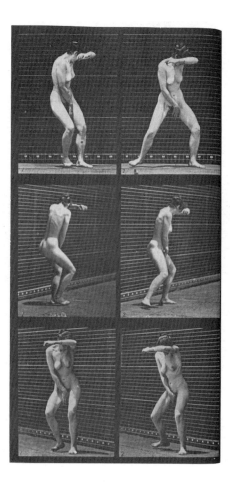

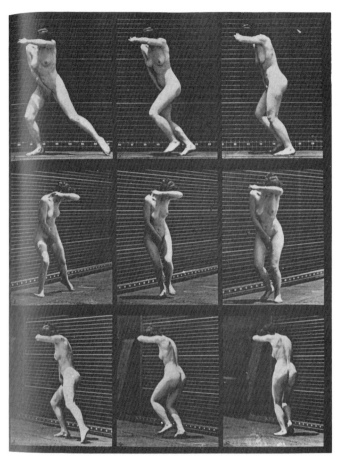

Catherine Aimer 'Turning around in surprise and running away', Plate 73, *Animal Locomotion*, 1887, collotype.

The women's movements are sometimes difficult to interpret. In many plates their long dresses hide their arms and legs, so that the muscular movement cannot be seen at all. The physiological laws that would be revealed by a photograph of Miss Coleman chasing Mrs Mitchell with a broom, or of Blanche Epler falling into a pile of hay, are impossible to fathom, and the scientific factors governing 'Fancy Dancing', the subject of Plates 187–9 and 191–4, are equally mysterious. In such pictures Muybridge's aesthetic and narrative requirements have triumphed over his commissioners' desire for analytically verifiable data. He has diverged from their interests to give us a treasure trove of figurative imagery, a reiteration of contemporary pictorial practice and a compendium of social history and erotic fantasy.

How much of this artful eroticism reflected Muybridge's repressed sexuality and personal longing for companionship, and how much his showman's instinct, is impossible to know. It had been eleven years since his brief marriage to Flora ended in humiliation. We are not aware of any other liaisons, and can only speculate about the relations he may have had with any of the models Mr Tadd found for him, or indeed with any other woman.

In the notebooks in which he recorded the photographic sessions, however, there is an entry for one with Blanche Epler. The session, the only one on 13 June, lasted six hours, and yielded but a single plate (426): 'Toilet, brushing her hair and walking off', shows the lovely Blanche from the front, back and side, nude, brushing her hair.

While the mule that takes off the professor's clothes and the trick ponies that ring bells and roll barrels would have been at home in the vaudeville acts and slide lectures that Muybridge and his audiences had seen, the female subjects participate in scenes the photographer creates: 'Walking in a gale', 'Crossing brook over a stepping stone', 'Woman kneels and drinks from the water jar of another woman and both walk off'. Few such images depict the activities of the modern American woman of 1885. Instead, Muybridge directs his models in fantasies from a distant pastoral age, as peasants and goddesses rake hay, play with fishing rods and raise antique water jugs to their shoulders. And, as the notebooks reveal, aside from the narrative arcs elicited by many single plates, even longer stories can be found by following the negatives' series numbers that show the order in which Muybridge photographed a particular model's movements. On 10 July 1885, for example, Catherine Aimer descends the stairs to pick up a pitcher, goes back up, sits, pours water into a glass from the pitcher, turns, runs (this is the print entitled 'Ashamed' in the notebooks and 'turning around in surprise and running away' in the published plate), runs again, picks up a basin and wipes it and then – perhaps tired from these activities – she lies down to read. Immediately after, she kneels with a basket, then with a bucket, and prepares to scrub.

The next day we find her sitting down again. She crosses her legs (this gesture seems important to Muybridge, as he bothers to note it), drinks from a cup, raises a 'Goblet' from the table, and then raises a pitcher and pours water from it. Next, perhaps to do something with the props Muybridge favours, she pours the water from the pitcher into a basin, washes her face and dries it. In a kind of free association, the basin becomes the cue for a dog to enter, and she feeds it. The basin is picked up and the water tossed out.

At this point the story falters, and Miss Aimer is reduced to throwing a baseball, walking with a fan and a jar, stumbling and falling, rising and sprinkling water (again, water is never far from the set). It is unclear what Muybridge might have meant her to do next. A soldier, a certain Mr Madison, was waiting in the wings to be photographed.

9

Final Years

On 16 March 1886 a reporter from *The Pennsylvanian* described the
work involved in preparing *Animal Locomotion* for publication:

> It will be accompanied by about twelve hundred plates, carbon
> reprints from the twenty-six thousand photographs already
> taken. Several hundred of the foremost scientists and educational
> institutions, both at home and abroad, are already subscribers.
>
> The working laboratories are in Biological Hall. In one, several
> assistants are constantly preparing the delicate photographic
> plates; in another, the developing etc. of the negatives is in
> process; and in another, presided over by a pretty young lady
> with a wealth of golden hair, the multitudinous plates are
> arranged and classified. Here is seen the unique zoopraxiscope
> for the reproduction of the actual locomotion from photographs.
>
> Mr Muybridge looks and talks like a philosopher. He is a
> genial gentleman in the prime of life, and, although his beard is
> long and white, and hair and eyebrows shaggy, his countenance
> is ruddy, clean-cut and intellectual. He is intensely enthusiastic in
> his work, and takes a genuine pleasure in explaining his theories
> and apparatus to interested friends.

In September, with the printing well underway, Edward Coates,
the chair of the scientific committee, proposed a meeting with
Pepper and the other members. The ambitious agenda included

examining the 781 plates; considering the contracts and copyrights; going over a new subscription circular with 500 names; reviewing 'Muybridge's catalogue' and the 'treatises by Parker, Allen, Eakins, Muybridge and French'; and deciding on whether a time record should be printed on each plate. Coates also raised an alarm concerning the 562 human figures that would be shown and whether the nudity would pass muster:

> If the work is to be published at all the usual question as to the study of the nude in Art and Science must be answered Yes. Otherwise the greater number of the 562 series would be excluded. At the same time there are probably some lines to be drawn with regard to some of the plates. That there will be objections in some quarters to the publication would seem to be most likely if not inevitable.[1]

Small wonder Coates was concerned. Of the 562 human bodies in *Animal Locomotion*, 340 of them were naked. And even if a good part of the male nudity could be justified by the need to see clearly the muscular changes produced by particular movements in sports or other actions, the erotic and transgressive acts engaged in by the naked female models (or, for that matter, even the farces and jokes they participated in while clothed, or the antics of the animals) could not be so easily integrated into the sort of publication benefiting science and art that the committee envisaged. Moreover, public opinion in 1880s Philadelphia had been swayed by the anti-vice crusade of Josiah W. Leeds, who led a public-relations campaign against immoral behaviour, prurient images and obscene literature. In 1885 a group of self-appointed moral guardians called the Citizen's Representative Committee of Philadelphia insisted on the arrest and imprisonment of persons who threatened moral principles, and that year Leeds had a theatre owner arrested for posting pictures of women in tights. Coates's dismissal of Eakins from the Academy of the Fine Arts in 1886 is thought to be one of the outcomes of Leeds's campaign. In March 1887, just as *Animal Locomotion* was being finalized for publication, Leeds succeeded in getting a law passed that prohibited lewd pictures, 'defined as representations of the human form in nude or semi-nude condition' but 'not to be confused with purely scientific works written on the subject of sexual physiology or works of art'. Photographs, however, were not included in the latter category.[2]

Surprisingly, the wrath of the anti-vice crusaders hardly touched Muybridge's photographs. Quite the contrary: they were praised in the press and in popular journals, and the work as a whole was lauded internationally as a contribution to science and art. There are many reasons for this. The project was funded as an objective investigation of movement; the plates were made with the camera, which now, much more so than earlier in the century, was accepted as an objective (because mechanical) instrument of science; as described in the previous chapter, the images were published in an order and format that conformed to a typical scientific atlas of the period; and the gridded background in individual images bestowed a scientific aura on the contents. Furthermore, Muybridge's *Prospectus and Catalogue*, which functioned as both a preview and an order form, bore the imprimatur of the University of Pennsylvania on its very first page, followed by a lengthy and detailed description of the arrangement and methodology of the work. The catalogue section was completely bland. Each plate identified the state of dress or undress of each subject, so a prospective purchaser would know exactly what he or she was getting; the plates were given innocuous titles that described only the movement; and the models were never mentioned by name, only by number and short description. A space was given to the subscriber to check off any number of plates for a dollar each; to choose a selection of 100 plates, to be bound in leather, for $100; or, for the serious collector, to purchase the entire eleven portfolios of

781 plates for $600. Most important, the social and professional status of the individual members of the committee – all except Eakins were upper-class Philadelphians – and the rising reputation of the university were the ultimate factors that allowed the work to pass as an objective, disinterested and accurate study of animal locomotion.[3]

Although Muybridge told a reporter from *The Pennsylvanian* on 28 September 1886 that he had written a lengthy introduction and that 'his colleague Dr Andrew J. Parker' (a professor of physics at the university who had modelled for Muybridge) was 'at work on the descriptive text for the plates', neither of those essays, nor the one promised by Eakins, appeared in *Animal Locomotion*. Within a year of the publication of the work, the university issued a companion volume of essays written by three committee members: William Marks, Harrison Allen and Dr Dercum. All three damned Muybridge's work indirectly. Marks and Dercum emphasized the advantage of Marey's single-camera as 'yielding a means of measurement as near scientifically exact and free from sources of error as we can hope to reach'.[4] Allen wrote that many of the statements in his essay 'could have been deduced from data already accessible to the writer but since he wrote the paper immediately after the inspection of the photographs his conclusion may be said to be based on them', and Pepper in his introduction to the essays noted that 'the mass of novel material represented in this work is so great that it has not as yet been possible to subject any considerable portion of it to critical examination',[5] an attitude shared by most writers on *Animal Locomotion* until quite recently.

In the fall of 1888 Muybridge – now almost always referred to in news reports as 'Professor Muybridge' – had new zoopraxiscope discs made from the *Animal Locomotion* photographs and began to lecture again, with the particular purpose of promoting the work and finding more subscribers to offset its costs. In update letters to Pepper's secretary Jesse Burk, Muybridge often included a tally:

'I did pretty well in Chicago. 14 ($100) subscribers and 2 complete series ($600 each) and expect some more when I return.'[6]

The work received a great deal of attention, both good and bad, in the press. The *Philadelphia Evening Telegraph* warned its readers that while the plates were beautiful, they were also curious and some of them 'it needs to be said, at least approach a line of sensationalism beyond which the dignities disappear, and the propriety of offering some of the plates to subscribers may reasonably be doubted'.[7] But the more sophisticated New York papers typically impressed upon readers the photographs' importance for art. In a lengthy review on 10 January 1888 the *New York Nation* called for the work to be in 'in every scientific and artistic institution in the country and in the world', and reminded readers that Muybridge's investigations 'began in the attempt to demonstrate the falsity of some commonly accepted and traditional methods of depicting the gaits of the horse'. As for the nudity of the human subjects, it was found to be acceptable: it had been done for a higher cause:

> Here for the first time, human eyes may see just how the human body moves in the performance of its functions . . . This is not an art, but it is a mine of facts of nature that no artist can afford to neglect. How would Signorelli, that enthusiast of movement and anatomy who drew his dead son naked, or Michael Angelo or Benvenuto have revelled in such volumes as these . . . How splendid nature is! Here are dancing girls graceful enough to delight the soul of Raphael . . . [The artist] may even do well to throw away his photographs altogether, the action once understood, and express it by a pose not actually found in any one of them, but conveying better than any of them, taken separately, the total results of the series. For the end of art is not record but expression.

In interviews, Muybridge also emphasized the utility of the images for artists who, by studying the plates 'representing the integral and consecutive elements of one completed action . . . [would] be enabled to analyze this action more thoroughly and accurately than would be possible in the study of nature unaided by the camera. In this way they would certainly avoid some errors into which they are now prone to fall.' But he also stressed the aspect of scientific discovery. 'The most interesting and the most valuable discovery I made during my whole investigation was the similarity of locomotion in all animals. This fact has not been recognized before but that it is demonstrable my plates incontrovertibly prove.' And he was always happy to explain some of the plates to reporters. He describes the plate in which Catherine Aimer pours a bucket of water over Mrs Cooper as the result of a desire – we're not told whose –

> to show the affect upon the muscles of a sudden shock; so a woman was seated in a tub and another one emptied a bucket of water upon her. But some of my assistants, in the spirit of fun, dissolved a lump of ice in the water just before it was used. The model had not counted upon this, and she sprang out crying, 'Oh, I cannot stand it'. If we had tried we could not have produced a more satisfactory effect. Artists say that her attitude as she stands shivering and seeking to throw the water off is perfect.[8]

Muybridge's new pictures created a dilemma for some artists, just as his photographs of Stanford's horses had. His cameras captured what the eye could not see. What, then, should the artist who depended on the camera as guarantor of the visible do with them? 'A picture should represent what we see', wrote one critic, and '[Muybridge] would be the first to admit that the eye cannot properly be said to see any one of the attitudes he has shown to be really assumed by the galloping horse'.[9]

Academic artists, who held that being true to nature was more important than following artistic convention, on the other hand, were the most interested in and the most affected by what Muybridge's camera revealed. For them, this simply extended the reach of the 'visible' world to be imitated in their art; they studied the pictures and adjusted their representations accordingly. Meissonier, for example, who had been so struck by Muybridge's photographs of horses, copied his famous battle picture *Friedland 1807* (1875) in watercolour in March 1887, changing the positions of the horses to conform to the photographs. Meissonnier's friends Alexandre Cabanel and Jean-Léon Gérôme, who had both been present at his soirée for Muybridge in 1881, also integrated what the photographs showed into their depictions of animals. Edgar Degas used the photographs in a more complex way than just copying the positions. He made two drawings from Plate 620; *Canter, saddle, thoroughbred bay mare Annie G.* and used the photographs as a basis for his wax models of horses, but more significant, he composed paintings of dancers that effectively dissolved Muybridge's lateral and foreshortened frames to show the different positions of a single figure, sometimes overlaying them in dynamic laminates and sometimes separating them in a frieze.

For other artists, the photographs opened the first unavoidable schism between art and science. 'It is the artist who is truthful and it is photography which lies', wrote Auguste Rodin, 'for in reality time does not stop and if the artist succeeds in producing the impression of a movement which takes several moments for accomplishment, his work is certainly much less conventional than the scientific image, where time is abruptly suspended.'[10]

Muybridge himself took part in these discussions only to the extent that he continued to give slide lectures comparing the accuracy with which artists throughout history had represented horses' gaits with the results provided by his photographs. Such was the beginning of a series of lectures he gave in Orange, New Jersey, starting on 25 February 1888 before a packed house. After the slide demonstration, he used his zoopraxiscope to illustrate the movements of different animals, including lions, elephants, camels, kangaroos and dogs, followed by scantily clad men and women, boxers and 'a series of pictures of female dancers pirouetting, which called down repeated applause'.[11] One outraged audience member complained in a letter to the *Orange Journal* about the emphasis given to pictures of the 'sporting world' (at the time, boxing was outlawed in many parts of the u.s.) and questioned 'the propriety of exhibiting semi-nude figures at a promiscuous assembly' given that it would provide a 'shock to the delicate sensibilities . . . Among savages such exhibitions are natural and expected but in civilized society they are shocking to the moral sentiment, indecent and demoralizing.'[12]

On 27 February Muybridge visited the noted inventor Thomas Edison at his West Orange laboratory, purportedly to talk over the possibility of combining the zoopraxiscope with Edison's invention, the phonograph. The 2 June *New York World* gave an account of the meeting:

Prof. Muybridge claimed to have almost perfected a photographic appliance by which he would be enabled to accurately reproduce the gestures and facial expression of a man making speech. This was done, he said by taking some sixty or seventy instantaneous photographs of each position assumed by the speaker and then throwing them by means of a magic lantern upon a screen. He proposed to Mr Edison that the phonograph should be used in connection with his invention, and that the photographs of Edwin Booth as Hamlet, Lillian Russell in some of her songs, and other artists of note should be experimented with. Mr Edison, he said, could produce with his instrument the tones of the voice while he would furnish the gestures and facial expression. This scheme met with the approval of Mr Edison and he intended to perfect it at his leisure.

Edison quickly realized the limitations of Muybridge's silhouettes and the zoopraxiscope mechanism, but he was evidently inspired by the visit nonetheless. By October, he had filed a caveat for his own motion-picture machine, the 'kinetoscope, an instrument which does for the Eye what the phonograph does for the Ear'.[13] During the first decade of the twentieth century, however, in his fight to control the burgeoning motion-picture industry in America, Edison would deny Muybridge's contribution and insist that the idea for motion pictures was entirely his own.

Muybridge continued to lecture through the summer and fall of 1888, in the Midwest as well as in Boston, New York and Philadelphia. In May 1889 he returned to England where, at Burlington House in London on 8 May, he lectured to the very Royal Society which had rejected him seven years earlier. The front page of the *Illustrated London News* featured an engraving of him lecturing in front of a lantern slide and included other engravings made from his photographs. In August he gave a demonstration before the Photographic Convention of Great Britain in an overcrowded hall in London; the *British Journal of Photography* on 23 August reported that he 'brought down the house'.

Muybridge embarked on an extended tour, appearing before sold-out audiences all over England, from Sheffield to Bristol and from Berkshire to Yorkshire.[14] A report from Ipswich on 3 February 1890 describes a lecture that ran for nearly two hours, where Muybridge played the role of both scientist and entertainer. He analyzed the movements of the animals that appeared to gallop before his audience at great speed by showing them a second time in slow motion. Then, with his 'dry humour', he called attention to the most 'laughable pictures of all, those of a kicking mule – the best kicker that could be got hold of'.[15]

'Mr Muybridge Showing his Instantaneous Photographs of Animal Motion at the Royal Society', *The Illustrated London News*, 25 May 1889.

Throughout the spring of 1890, he lectured in Scotland and Ireland; in August he visited New York, but by late fall he was back lecturing in Bristol, Dundee, Birmingham and Manchester. In January 1891 he turned up in Paris, where he spoke on the 'Science of Animal Locomotion in Relation to Design in Art' at the Hôtel de la Société de Géographie before a 'brilliant audience, which included

a large number of the most distinguished artists in Paris'.[16] On 9
March, in Berlin, he began a tour of Germany. The reception was
less enthusiastic.

Berlin audiences were already familiar with a machine that
was taking Europe by storm, Ottomar Anschütz's *Schnellseher*, or
'quick viewer'. In 1885, inspired by German reports of Muybridge's
1881–2 lectures, Anschütz had devised a multiple camera system that
incorporated focal-plane shutters to produce the sharpest images
then on the market. His *Schnellseher* held 24 transparencies of his
sequence photographs arranged around the rim of a disc; as each
transparency passed in front of a projecting lens, flashes of light
from a Geissler tube illuminated them in turn, a stroboscopic
effect that produced the impression of continuous movement.
Some 19,000 people had seen the *Schnellseher* at the Paris Universal
Exposition in 1887, and Muybridge, too, would already have been
aware of it – the *Philadelphia Photographer* had carried a report on
4 June 1887. Perhaps unbeknownst to Muybridge, that same August in
New York projections were given with the device under the name
'Electrotachyscope'. It was also featured in the 14 October *New York
Times* and on the front page of the November 1887 issue of *Scientific
American*. In the German press, Muybridge's work had usually been
compared unfavourably to Anschütz's.[17] Now, on Muybridge's
arrival in Berlin, Bruno Meyer, reporting in the *Deutsches Photographen-Zeitung*, criticized both the man and his work. He took
Muybridge to task for lecturing in English – a translator had
appeared with him only on the first evening – and though the
American's 'dignified and impressive personality' won everyone
over, wrote Meyer, his 'colloquially pronounced backwoods English
must have worked to repulse'. The reviewer criticized Muybridge's
art slides for their lack of clarity, and while praising the slides
of human movement taken simultaneously from three points
of view, saw that they were disadvantaged owing to the small
number of phases of movement they contained. Though Meyer

acknowledged Muybridge as a pioneer in stop-action photography, he considered his work now sadly out-of-date. As for the zoopraxi-scope projections, Meyer found the images were the same silhouettes Muybridge had shown years earlier and lamented that someone who had 'set the pace of research work so significantly . . . could come to squander the experience with this: inadequate even as a child's entertainment'.[18]

We have no record of Muybridge's response to this attack. It was probably nugatory: his ego had withstood such criticisms before. Leaving Berlin he once again found the kind of appreciative audiences and laudatory press accounts he was used to. He lectured in Munich and other towns in southern Germany, and then in Rome, Naples, Turin and Switzerland. He also continued to gain subscribers to his work. Returning to Berlin on 15 July, Muybridge wrote to Jesse Burk for 200 copies of the *Prospectus and Catalogue of Plates*, recounting his travels and sales. He had secured the 'French Academy and the International Society of Artists' as subscribers, he said, as well as those of 'nearly all the universities in Italy, Switzerland and South Germany' and, as he put it, he 'obtained for the University of Pennsylvania a recognition of its enlightened and liberal policy'. Furthermore, he told Burk, he had found to his surprise that there were 'few painters of any great distinction' in Rome. Nonetheless, he had taken some holidays, climbing Vesuvius and wandering through the 'once animated streets of Pompeii'. Meyer's remarks about his English might have touched a nerve, for in describing his lecture in Turin, he wrote, 'I am happy to say that I now speak Italian, German and French with equal fluency. Professor [Angelo] Mosso [Marey's friend and physiology collaborator] however, very kindly rendered my remarks to the audience in his own admirable style, as I was not quite familiar with the *Turin* dialect.'[19]

In November Muybridge returned to Philadelphia to prepare a new work for publication, a pamphlet called *The Science of Animal*

Locomotion (Zoopraxography): An Electro-Photographic Investigation of Consecutive Phases of Animal Movements in which he listed all the subscribers he had so far collected. In spring 1892 he journeyed west to give a series of lectures in San Francisco. There he wrote to David Jordan, the president of the newly created Stanford University, founded in 1891 as a memorial to Leland Jr, who had died in Florence in 1884 of typhus. Muybridge suggested to Jordan that the university might be interested in supporting investigations he wished to undertake on the subject of flight. On 5 April he wrote again to offer his services 'for one, or a course of Lectures' because, Muybridge expressed, he would be gratified to give his lecture in the place where his first experiments were made. But no invitation was forthcoming; it became clear that there was no future for him at Stanford. In one last attempt, he decided to petition Stanford himself – now a u.s. senator. He drafted a letter on 2 May in which he went over the history of their relationship, stressing the disaster caused to him by Stillman's publication. He concluded that he had 'patiently waited during eleven years without bringing this matter to your attention, but I think that the time has arrived when in justice both to you and to myself I ought to do so'.[20] We don't know whether Stanford ever received the letter. Muybridge also wrote to his former patron in the hope of reclaiming some boxes of equipment, which he had left there in 1881. Stanford never released the boxes; he died on 21 June 1893, leaving it to his estate to return Muybridge's possessions.

Before he left San Francisco, Muybridge saw Floredo, now eighteen years old and caring for animals on a ranch. Muybridge's deep ambivalence about this young man was not altered by the meeting. He judged the boy limited and lacking any ambition to better himself and decided to end the financial support he had been providing the years he was away. He transferred the remaining money he had on account for Floredo in San Francisco to his cousins in Kingston, handed him a gold watch and a picture of himself, and never saw him again.

While in California, preparing for a tour to Asia, Muybridge received an invitation from the Fine Arts Commission to set up a venue at the Chicago World's Columbian Exposition in which to lecture and give zoopraxiscope demonstrations. He was expected to pay for the building (it would cost $6,000), but could offset the expense by charging admission and selling his photographs. Accepting the invitation, Muybridge began to have a new set of discs produced, this time in colour. Twelve inches (30.5 cm) in diameter, the colours were painted onto photographs of outline drawings – a rather onerous process – by Erwin F. Faber, a Philadelphia medical illustrator.

Muybridge's Zoopraxographical Hall, situated on the Midway Plaisance – the ancestor of all carnival Midways – was a 50 × 80 feet (15 × 24 m) construction of wood and iron faced in brick. Its wide portico was supported by two ornate columns, and Muybridge's performances were announced by the raising of banners as well as by broadsides. The first building ever constructed in which to show moving pictures to a paying public, the Hall opened on the Midway in the summer of 1893.

In Chicago Muybridge perfectly meshed his role of entrepreneur and showman. Hoping to reach larger and more diverse audiences than ever before, he gave slide lectures and zoopraxiscope demonstrations with both the new and old discs, sold boxes of 'fifty beautifully printed cards' made for the phenakistoscope with images on them drawn from the Philadelphia work by Faber, 'Zoopraxiscopic fans', and a selection of twelve coloured and preperforated discs. For the occasion he had even produced a new version of *Descriptive Zoopraxography* in a larger edition with more illustrations.

The venture, unfortunately, was not a commercial success. Muybridge's advertisement for his presentations stressed the educational aspect of his work ('the present series of Lectures may not be unworthy of the attention of the Philosopher') over any entertainment appeal, though he did try to downplay the 'technicalities' in an attempt to reach 'popular and juvenile audiences'. To make matters worse, he emphasized the lectures as being under the auspices of the u.s. Government Board of Education and the University of Pennsylvania – not a promising way to compete with the other Midway attractions.

And they were many. Under the viaducts, Anschütz's machine was showing animated photographs of the same subjects hawked explicitly as amusement. Not far away, the very first Ferris wheel was circling over the crowds, and a belly dancer, a flesh-and-blood exotic dancer, not a photographed or animated one, was appearing daily to perform the 'hootchy-kootchy' dance. Muybridge's profit for the sale of his side items was $213.43 for the entire period to 31 October, when his contract ended. Anschütz took in $1,472.

Rather than abandon his machine, however, Muybridge continued to have new discs made. In the spring he had Faber paint a sequence featuring the Derby and carried it and the other discs to England, the scene of his last triumph. He arrived in September 1894, staying first with a cousin in his grandmother's house in Hampton Wick. In spring 1895, from a new address in Kingston, he published *The Motion of the Horse and Other Animals in Nature and in Art*, a pamphlet that announced a lecture tour from October to March and promised 40 new zoopraxiscopic projecting discs.

With the advent of cinema – Anschütz's projections had been seen in London since 1894, and the first projections of motion pictures on film lasting a minute or more had taken place in America, France and Germany by December 1895 – Muybridge's stellar career as a showman-lecturer came to an end. Although he would continue to give educational slide lectures, his zoopraxiscope, once considered a wonder machine, was by 1896 a historical curiosity.[21] Neither Muybridge nor his contemporaries could have foreseen that his brightly coloured discs, with their fantasy images of twirling dancers, crowds waving on racing horses, herds of buffalo chased by Indians and monkeys clambering up coconut palms, anticipated a completely different kind of animated medium: cartoons.

Ever the entrepreneur, Muybridge had already envisaged another venture, the last and most successful of his career: he would marry his 'dead' media to a new technology, the halftone process, to create yet another kind of narrative. Patented in America in 1893 and used increasingly in newspapers and illustrated journals at the turn of the century, the halftone allowed photographs to supplant woodblock prints in the illustrated press and made possible the rotogravure and the modern picture magazine. Muybridge decided to reissue his *Animal Locomotion* photographs as halftones in book form. He had a new audience in mind: the reader.

He presented the idea first to the University of Pennsylvania; but a fresh crisis occurred that made it impossible for the institution to subsidize him. The New York Photogravure Company, which had printed and stored the *Animal Locomotion* plates, was demanding payment for its printing costs and unsold prints, threatening destruction of the negatives and prints it held. Letters and telegrams between Muybridge and the now retired William Pepper flew back and forth. In June 1896 Muybridge set sail for America for the last time to resolve the problem. He arrived just in time to hear of the Photogravure's bankruptcy and the seizure of its assets – including his pictures. After a new, frantic exchange of telegrams with Pepper, Muybridge negotiated a solution. For $500 Pepper would receive the remaining complete sets of *Animal Locomotion* as well as the negatives and approximately 2,000 loose prints. He would put the proceeds of any sales towards the payment of the guarantors' original outlays; then, and only then, would Muybridge be reimbursed, although he would maintain the rights to make prints from the negatives.

The crisis over, Muybridge returned permanently to England in May 1897 to begin negotiations with the London publisher

Model 1 (Mrs Cooper) and Model 8 (Catherine Aimer) in 'Various Acts of Motion' from *The Human Figure in Motion*, 1901.

Chapman & Hall. *Animals in Motion: An Electro-Photographic Investigation of Consecutive Phases of Animal Progressive Movements*, the first volume of pictures derived from *Animal Locomotion*, was published in 1899. With its publication, and with Muybridge's ever more keen awareness that his zoopraxiscope might be viewed by history as a failed attempt at a motion-picture machine, he wrote on 16 June 1899 to Erwin Faber, directing him to go to Colt's in New York and with his own hands destroy the negatives of his drawings:

> I do not care for any lantern discs ever to be made from them, and I do not think it should be advisable that they should be any longer existant. I now much regret having ever made them, as they are not calculated to enhance my reputation, the original figures photographed from life, are those I prefer to leave behind

Models 4, 7, 12 and 15 displaying 'Miscellaneous Acts of Motion' from *The Human Figure in Motion*.

me, and I shall feel more comfortable when you write me of your having completely destroyed them.[22]

In 1901 Chapman & Hall published a second volume, *The Human Figure in Motion: An Electro-Photographic Investigation of Consecutive Phases of Muscular Actions*. Both volumes sold well, going into seven editions. They contain a preface by Muybridge, a selection of reduced sequences from *Animal Locomotion* and a section he titled 'Miscellaneous Phases . . . Selected from Various Seriates; and Reproduced on the Same Scale as Originally Published in *Animal Locomotion*'.

It is in these 'Miscellaneous Phases' that we see the final articulation of Muybridge's aesthetic vision. Here the logic of the sequence has been almost completely abandoned. Muybridge has chosen images from different sequences and organized them on the page into dynamic layouts. In them, each single picture affects the reading of the one next to it, or above or below it, enabling the reader to focus both on the spectacular nature of the gesture and pose in each and the relationships among them.

In the *Human Figure in Motion* we again find the pictures of men and women interacting with water, buckets and basins, which had appeared so frequently in *Animal Locomotion*. But in this last incarnation of his project, Muybridge points to a new context for his models – the modern magazine; and he addresses a new viewer – the modern reader rifling through the pages in no particular order, stopping and starting at will, seeking not just information but the kind of visual pleasure that Muybridge had always known how to provide.

After so peripatetic and tumultuous a life, Muybridge spent his last years living tranquilly with his cousins in Kingston. Whatever disappointment he might have felt over the fact that his zoopraxi-scope had been eclipsed by motion-picture technology, his place in the history of photography was secure. Like Marey's, Muybridge's revolutionary photographic dissections have permanently altered our perceptions of space and time.

Muybridge died in Kingston on 8 May 1904 of prostate cancer. Legend has it that he was naked when he died, digging a scale model of the Great Lakes in his garden.

References

1 Kingston to California

1 Maybanke Susannah Anderson, 'My Sprig of Rosemary', in Jan Roberts, ed., *Maybanke: A Woman's Voice: The Collected Work of Maybanke Selfe-Wolstenholme-Anderson, 1845–1927*, ed. Jan Roberts and Beverley Kingston (Sydney, 2000), p. 25.
2 Anderson, 'My Sprig of Rosemary', p. 17.
3 Ibid., p. 18.
4 Ibid., p. 25.
5 Official catalogue of the *Great Exhibition of the Works of Industry of All Nations* (London, 1851).
6 *Illustrated London News*, 18 (1851), p. 485.
7 Anderson, 'My Sprig of Rosemary', p. 25.
8 Selleck, testimony at Muybridge's murder trial, *San Francisco Chronicle*, 4 February 1875.
9 The census for the city in 1852 is 34,776; in 1860, 56,802.
10 Philip J. Ethington, *The Public City: The Political Construction of Urban Life in San Francisco, 1850–1900* (Cambridge and New York, 1994).
11 Robert Bartlett Haas, *Muybridge: Man in Motion* (Berkeley, CA, 1976), p. 6.
12 *Daily Alta California*, 18 January 1859.
13 *Daily Alta California*, 13 December 1858.
14 (San Francisco) *Daily Evening Post*, 6 February 1875.
15 Gull is the Ripper in a number of books: *From Hell*, by writer Alan Moore and artist Eddie Campbell; Iain Sinclair's *White Chappell, Scarlet Tracings*; and 'Royal Blood', a storyline in issues 52–5 of the Vertigo Comics series *Hellblazer*, written by Garth Ennis. See also Melvyn

Fairclough, *The Ripper and the Royals* (London, 1991). However, Gull was in his seventies and had suffered a stroke by the time the murders began so he is an unlikely suspect.

16 Muybridge to Henry Selfe, 17 August 1861, cited in Haas, *Muybridge*, p. 10.

17 *Daily Alta California*, 3 December 1862.

18 Stephen Herbert discovered Muybridge's activities as a venture capitalist. See www.stephenherbert.co.uk/muy%20blog.htm#part1 (accessed 12 May 2010).

2 Helios in America

1 Unsigned, in 'Leland Stanford's Gift to Art and to Science', *San Francisco Examiner*, 6 February 1881.

2 *Philadelphia Photographer*, November 1869.

3 Peter E. Palmquist, *Carleton E. Watkins: Photographer of the American West* (Fort Worth, TX and Albuquerque, NM, 1983), pp. 18–19.

4 Mary V. Jessup Hood and Robert Bartlett Haas, 'Eadweard Muybridge's Yosemite Valley Photographs, 1867–1872', *California Historical Society Quarterly*, 43 (March 1963), p. 9.

5 These can be seen online in his studio sample book at www.oac.cdlib.org/findaid/ark:/13030/tf6t1nb6w7 (accessed 12 May 2010).

6 *Philadelphia Photographer*, April 1866.

7 Described in *Philadelphia Photographer*, 5 May 1869.

8 Helen Hunt Jackson, *Bits of Travel at Home* (Boston, 1878), p. 86. Jackson's original review was published in the New York *Independent*, 29 August 1872.

9 Ellis Paxson Oberholtzer, *A History of the United States since the Civil War*, 5 vols (New York, 1917), vol. I, p. 123.

10 *Daily Evening Bulletin*, 9 October 1869, p. 3.

11 Halleck to Muybridge, 13 October 1868. National Archives, Washington, DC, cited in *Daily Evening Bulletin*, 17 October 1868.

12 *Alaska Herald*, 9 July 1872, Scrapbook, Kingston Museum.

13 Robert Bartlett Haas, *Muybridge: Man in Motion* (Berkeley, CA, 1976), p. 24.

14 Rebecca Solnit, *River of Shadows: Eadweard Muybridge and the Technological Wild West* (New York, 2003), p. 58.

15 Mead B. Kibbey, *The Railroad Photographs of Alfred A. Hart, Artist* (Sacramento, CA, 1996).

16 Philip J. Ethington, *The Public City: The Political Construction of Urban Life in San Francisco, 1850–1900* (Cambridge and New York, 1994), p. 155.

3 The Wild Wild West

1 *Daily Evening Bulletin*, 19 October 1874.

2 Muybridge to Col. R. S. Williamson, Lighthouse Board, 13 January 1871. Lighthouse Board letter book, National Archives and Records Administration, Washington, DC.

3 *Catalogue of Photographic Views Illustrating the Yosemite, Mammoth Trees, Geyser Springs, and Other Remarkable and Interesting Scenery of the Far West by Muybridge* (San Francisco, CA, 1873), p. 37.

4 Helen Hunt Jackson, *Bits of Travel at Home* (Boston, 1878; 2nd edn, 1880), p. 86.

5 Cited in Anita Mozley, ed., *Eadweard Muybridge: The Stanford Years, 1872–1882*, revd edn (Stanford, CA, 1973), p. 8.

6 *Daily Alta California*, 30 August 1877. Scrapbook 19, Kingston Museum.

7 *Philadelphia Photographer*, March 1879.

8 *Journal of the Franklin Institute*, April 1883.

9 Muybridge, introduction to *Animals in Motion*, 5th edn (London, 1925), p. 13.

10 Scrapbook, p. 7, Kingston Museum.

11 (New York) *Independent*, 29 August 1872.

12 'Photographic Studies', *Alta California*, 7 April 1873.

13 Ibid.

14 Paul Hickman and Terence Pitts, 'On the Life and Photographic Works of George Fiske', in *George Fiske, Yosemite Photographer* (Flagstaff, AZ, 1980), p. 21. Hickman feels that Fiske joined Muybridge's 'caravan of pack mules for at best part of the summer and that they probably photographed the giant sequoias of Mariposa Grove together'. Ibid.

15 *Daily Evening Bulletin*, 17 January 1872.

16 Peter Palmquist, Lawrence and Thomas Housseworth and Co.: *A Unique View of the West*, 1860–1886 (Columbus, OH, 1980), p. 36.

17 *Catalogue of Photographic Views Illustrating the Yosemite, Mammoth Trees,*

Geyser Springs, and Other Remarkable and Interesting Scenery of the Far West by Muybridge (San Francisco: Bradley & Rulofson Gallery of Portrait and Landscape Photographic Art, 1873), p. 1.

18 *Daily Evening Bulletin*, 26 November 1873.

19 Erwin N. Thompson, *The Modoc War: Its Military History and Topography* (Sacramento, CA, 1971), p. 141.

4 Love, Loss and Central America

1 *San Francisco Chronicle*, 19 October 1874.

2 *Sacramento Daily Union*, 8 February 1875.

3 *San Francisco Chronicle*, 21 December 1874.

4 *San Francisco Chronicle*, 6 February 1875

5 *Sacramento Daily Union*, 5 February 1875.

6 *San Francisco Chronicle*, 20 October 1874.

7 *San Francisco Chronicle*, 21 October 1874.

8 *Napa Register* (weekly edition), 13 February 1875.

9 *Sunday Chronicle*, 7 February 1875.

10 *Sacramento Daily Union*, 8 February 1875.

11 *San Francisco Chronicle*, 23 March 1875.

12 'Mrs Muybridge Brings Suit for Divorce and Makes Additional Allegations', *Sacramento Daily Union*, 1 April 1875.

13 *Sacramento Daily Union*, 1 May 1875.

14 *San Francisco Post*, 10 November 1876.

15 E. Bradford Burns, *Eadweard Muybridge in Guatemala, 1875: The Photographer as Social Recorder* (Berkeley, CA, 1986).

16 *Panama Star*, 1 May [1875], Scrapbook, p. 14, Kingston Museum.

17 Scrapbook, p. 15, insert, Kingston Museum.

18 *Panama Star*, 1 November 1875.

19 Ellsworth Westervelt, 'A Trip to Central America', *Scribner's Monthly*, XV/5 (March 1878), pp. 609–24.

20 Eadweard Muybridge papers, 1876–1955. Series Title / No.: BANC MSS C-B 715 Pt II positive microfilm Bancroft Library.

21 *Report of the Eleventh Industrial Exhibition under the Auspices of the Mechanics' Institute of the City of San Francisco* (San Francisco, CA, 1876), p. 226.

5 Panoramic San Francisco

1 Robert Louis Stevenson, 'A Modern Cosmopolis', *Magazine of Art*, January 1883, p. 275.

2 Ibid., p. 276.

3 Eric Sandweiss, 'Claiming the Urban Landscape: The Improbable Rise of an Inevitable City', in David Harris, with Eric Sandweiss, *Eadweard Muybridge and the Photographic Panorama of San Francisco, 1850–1880* (Montreal and London, 1993), p. 31.

4 Diana Strazdes, 'The Millionaire's Palace: Leland Stanford's Commission for Pottier & Stymus in San Francisco', *Winterthur Portfolio*, XXXVI/4 (2001), pp. 213–42.

5 Ibid., p. 216.

6 *Stanford Alumnus*, 7 May 1906, p. 5.

7 The album is illustrated and the panorama described and reproduced in full in Harris, *Eadweard Muybridge and the Photographic Panorama*, pp. 103–5 and 108–9.

8 Martha Sandweiss, *Print the Legend: Photography and the American West* (New Haven, CT, and London, 2002), p. 57.

9 Ibid., p. 53.

10 Harris, *Eadweard Muybridge and the Photographic Panorama*, p. 37.

11 Ibid., p. 118.

12 Ibid., p. 38.

13 Ibid., p.120.

14 Ibid., p.118.

15 Prospectus from Morse's Gallery, September 1877, Scrapbook, Kingston Museum.

16 *Daily Alta California*, 22 July 1877.

17 Harris, *Eadweard Muybridge and the Photographic Panorama*, p. 50.

18 Muybridge sold two in 1897. For locations of the others, see ibid., p. 123.

19 *Daily Alta California*, 3 August 1877.

20 *Morning Call*, 10 August 1877.

6 Stopping Time on Stanford's Ranch

1 Étienne-Jules Marey, *Animal Mechanism: A Treatise on Terrestrial and Aerial Locomotion*, 2nd edn (London, 1874).

2 Ibid., p. 137.

3 Ibid., p. 178.

4 Muybridge to Poett, September 1877. Wilson Centre for Photography, London.

5 The number twelve might have been based on Oscar Gustave Rejlander's 'On Photographing Horses', *British Journal Photographic Almanac* (1872–3), p. 115.

6 Edward [*sic*] J. Muybridge v. Leland Stanford, Suffolk Superior Court, Massachusetts, Collis P. Huntington Collection, George Arents Research Library, Syracuse University.

7 Ibid.

8 Muybridge to Poett, Wilson Centre for Photography, London.

9 *Pacific Rural Press*, 22 June 1878.

10 J.D.B. Stillman, *The Horse in Motion as Shown by Instantaneous Photography, with a Study on Animal Mechanics Founded on Anatomy and the Revelation of the Camera in Which Is Demonstrated the Theory of Quadrupedal Locomotion* (Boston, 1882), p. 125.

11 Joel Snyder in conversation with the author.

12 *Sacramento Daily Union*, 18 June 1878.

13 *Pacific Rural Press*, 22 June 1878.

14 *Morning Call*, 16 June 1878. Scrapbook, p. 21, Kingston Museum.

15 *Morning Call*, 16 June 1878.

16 *Resources of California*, August 1878. Scrapbook, p.27, Kingston Museum.

17 *Examiner*, 1 July 1878.

18 *Resources of California*, August 1878. Scrapbook, p.27, Kingston Museum.

19 Receipt from Jero. L. Boone to Muybridge, 14 June 1878. Wilson Centre.

20 Charles Musser, *The Emergence of Cinema: The American Screen to 1907* (Berkeley, CA, 1990), p. 38.

21 Corey Keller, 'Magnificent Entertainment: The Spectacular Eadweard Muybridge', in *Helios: Eadweard Muybridge in a Time of Change*, exh. cat. ed. Philip Brookman, Corcoran Gallery of Art (Washington, DC, and Göttingen, 2010).

22 'A Horse's Motion Scientifically Determined', *Scientific American*
(19 October 1878), p. 241.

23 Marey to Tissandier, *La Nature*, 18 December 1878. My translation.

24 Muybridge to Tissandier, 17 February, published in *La Nature*, 22 March
1879, p. 246.

25 Cited by Lloyd Goodrich, *Thomas Eakins*, 2nd edn (Cambridge, MA,
1982), vol. 1, p. 263.

26 Ibid.

27 Stephen Herbert, ed., *Eadweard Muybridge: The Kingston Museum
Bequest* (Hastings, 2004), p. 110. On Muybridge zoetropes, see
www.stephenherbert.co.uk/muybZOETROPES.htm (accessed 14 May
2010).

7 Touring Europe

1 Stephen Herbert has done the most complete research on the zoopraxiscope. See Herbert, *Eadweard Muybridge: The Kingston Museum Bequest*
(Hastings, 2004).

2 Preface to Eadweard Muybridge, *Animals in Motion: An Electro-
Photographic Investigation of Consecutive Phases of Animal Progressive
Movements* (London, 1899), p. 3.

3 Herbert, *Eadweard Muybridge*, p. 113.

4 Muybridge, preface to *Animals in Motion*, p. 3.

5 Cited in Anita Mozley, ed., *Eadweard Muybridge: The Stanford Years,
1872–1882*, revd edn (Stanford, CA, 1973), p. 123.

6 Alex Olson has written on this album in 'Muybridge in the Parlor',
unpublished manuscript, 2008.

7 *Morning Call*, 9 May 1880, cited in Herbert, *Eadweard Muybridge*, p. 116.

8 Vallery Gréard, *Meissonier: His Life and His Art, with Extracts from His
Notebooks and His Opinions and Impressions on Art and Artists Collected
By His Wife* (London 1897), vol. II, p. 267.

9 'VAL', *Sacramento Daily Union*, 23 July 1881.

10 'Gov. Leland Stanford has gone to Europe.' *Pacific Rural Press*, 11 June
1881; Stanford in London according to *Sacramento Daily Union*, 16 June
1881.

11 Bill of Sale and Assignment, Leland Stanford to E. J. Muybridge, 30

May 1881. Bancroft Library University of California, Berkeley. Cited in
Anita Ventura Mozley, 'Introduction to the Dover Edition', in Eadweard
Muybridge, *Muybridge's Complete Human and Animal Locomotion: All 781
Plates from the 1887 Animal Locomotion* (Mineola, NY, 1979), vol. 1: xxiii.

12 *Le Globe*, Paris, 27 September 1881. English translation from the *San
Francisco Alta California*, 16 November 1881, Scrapbook, Kingston
Museum.

13 The painters included Bonnat, J. L. Gérôme, Edouard Détaille and
Alexandre Cabanel: Françoise Forster-Hahn, 'Marey, Muybridge and
Meissonier: The Study of Movement in Science and Art', in *Eadweard
Muybridge: The Stanford Years*, p. 85.

14 Muybridge to Frank Shay, 28 November 1881, Collis P. Huntington
Collection, George Arents Research Library, Syracuse University.

15 Étienne-Jules Marey, *La méthode graphique dans les sciences expérimen-
tales et principalement en physiologie et en médicine. Deuxième tirage
augmenté d'un supplément sur le développment de la méthode graphique
par la photographie* (Paris, 1885), p. 12.

16 Étienne-Jules Marey, *La Chronophotographie* (Conférence du
Conservatoire National des Arts et Métiers) (Paris, 1899), p. 8. For
similar views see Louis Gastine, *La Chronophotographie, sur plaque fixe
et sur pellicule mobile* (Paris, 1897), pp. 13ff and Joseph Eder, *La photographie instantanée* (Paris, 1888), chap. 21.

17 Muybridge to Shay, 23 December 1881, Collis P. Huntington Collection,
George Arents Research Library, Syracuse University.

18 Muybridge, transcript of letter to Marey, 19 January 1882, California
State Library, Sacramento, California.

19 'Mr Muybridge at the Royal Institution', *Photographic News*, XXVI/1228
(17 March 1882), p. 1.

20 Ibid.

21 See Rebecca Solnit, *River of Shadows: Eadweard Muybridge and the
Technological Wild West* (New York, 2003), pp. 271–2.

22 9 April 1882.

23 Muybridge to Stanford, 2 May 1892, Bancroft Library, University of
California, Berkeley.

24 Herbert, *Eadweard Muybridge*, p. 119.

25 Muybridge, transcript of letter to Marey, London, 30 May 1882.
California State Library, Sacramento.

26 Muybridge, transcript of letter to Marey, New York, 17 July 1882, California State Library, Sacramento.

27 E. J. Muybridge, *Prospectus of a New and Elaborate Work upon the Attitudes of Man, the Horse and Other Animals in Motion* (New York, 1883).

8 Making *Animal Locomotion*

1 William Pepper, 'Note', in W. D. Marks, H. Allen and F. X. Dercum, *Animal Locomotion: The Muybridge Work at the University of Pennsylvania – The Method and the Result* (Philadelphia, PA, 1888), p. 5.

2 'Mr Muybridge's Photographs: Interesting Pictures to Be Taken of Wild Birds and Beasts in Motion', *Philadelphia Ledger*, 12 August 1885.

3 Thomas Anschutz to J. Laurie Wallace, 18 June 1884. Archives of the Pennsylvania Academy of the Fine Arts, Philadelphia.

4 Thomas Anschutz to J. Laurie Wallace, August 1884. Archives of the Pennsylvania Academy of the Fine Arts, Philadelphia.

5 Anita Ventura Mozley, 'Introduction to the Dover Edition', in Eadweard Muybridge, *Muybridge's Complete Human and Animal Locomotion: All 781 Plates from the 1887 Animal Locomotion* (Mineola, NY, 1979), vol. 1, p. xxix.

6 Eadweard Muybridge, *Animal Locomotion: An Electro-Photographic Investigation of Consecutive Phases of Animal Movements*, 11 vols (Philadelphia, PA, 1887). Plates printed by the Photo-Gravure Company, New York, published under the auspices of the University of Pennsylvania.

7 Muybridge, *Prospectus and Catalogue of Plates*, p. 12.

8 Francis X. Dercum to G. E. Nitzsche, 20 May 1929. Gordon Hendricks Papers, Archives Center, National Museum of American History, Smithsonian Institution, Washington, DC.

9 William Pepper Memorandum, William Pepper papers, Collection of University Archives and Records Center, University of Pennsylvania, Philadelphia.

10 Frank Spencer, 'Some Notes on the Attempt to apply Photography to Anthropometry during the Second Half of the Nineteenth Century', in *Anthropology and Photography 1860–1920*, ed. Elizabeth Edwards (New Haven, CT, and London, 1992), p. 102.

11 'Animal Motion', *Philadelphia Times*, 2 August 1885.

9 Final Years

1 Coates to Pepper, Collection of University Archives and Records Center, University of Pennsylvania, Philadelphia.

2 Anne McCauley, '"The Most Beautiful of Nature's Works": Thomas Eakins's Photographic Nudes in their French and American Context', in *Eakins and the Photograph: Works by Thomas Eakins and his Circle in the Collection of the Pennsylvania Academy of the Fine Arts*, ed. Susan Danly and Cheryl Leibold (Washington, DC, 1994), pp. 54–5.

3 See Sarah Gordon, 'Out of Sequence: Suspended and Spectacular Bodies in Eadweard Muybridge's Animal Locomotion Series', *Spectator*, XXVIII/2 (Spring 2008), pp. 10–22.

4 William Dennis Marks, 'The Mechanism of Instantaneous Photography', in W. D. Marks, H. Allen and F. X. Dercum, *Animal Locomotion: The Muybridge Work at the University of Pennsylvania – The Method and the Result* (Philadelphia, PA, 1888), p. 15.

5 Ibid., pp. 35, 7.

6 Muybridge to Jesse Burk, 22 June 1888, Collection of University Archives and Records Center, University of Pennsylvania, Philadelphia.

7 *Philadelphia Evening Telegraph*, 15 August 1888.

8 *The Argus*, 13 March 1888, Scrapbook, Kingston Museum.

9 Richard A. Proctor, *Familiar Science Studies* (London, 1882).

10 August Rodin in conversation with Paul Gsell, cited in A. Scharf, *Art and Photography* (London and Baltimore, MD, 1968), p. 226.

11 *Orange* (NJ) *Chronicle*, 3 March 1888.

12 *Orange Journal*, cited in Charles Musser, *The Emergence of Cinema: The American Screen to 1907* (Berkeley, CA, 1990), p. 53.

13 Thomas Edison, Caveat 110, 8 October 1888, filed 17 October 1888. Patent records, Edison National Historic Site, West Orange, New Jersey.

14 A record of the lectures is in Stephen Herbert, ed., *Eadweard Muybridge: The Kingston Museum Bequest* (Hastings, 2004), pp. 127ff.

15 *East Anglian Daily Times*, 4 February 1890, cited in Herbert, *Eadweard Muybridge*, p. 150.

16 San Francisco *Daily Evening Bulletin*, 18 February 1891.

17 *Illustrierte Zeitung*, Leipzig, 1 January 1886 no. 2218, 21; Josef Maria Eder, *Jahrbuch für Photographie* (1887), p. 111.

18 Bruno Meyer, 'Muybridge in Berlin', *Deutsches Photographen-Zeitung*,

nos. 12, 14, 15 (1891); translation by Deac Rossell.

19 Muybridge to Burk, 15 July 1891, University Archives and Records Center, University of Pennsylvania, Philadelphia.

20 Muybridge to Stanford, 2 May 1892, Bancroft Library, University of California, Berkeley.

21 Herbert, *Eadweard Muybridge*, p. 138.

22 Muybridge to Faber, 16 June 1899, University Archives and Records Center, University of Pennsylvania, Philadelphia.

Select Bibliography

Works by Muybridge

Animal Locomotion: An Electro-Photographic Investigation of Consecutive Phases of Animal Movements, 1872–1885, 11 vols, 781 plates (Philadelphia, 1887)

Animal Locomotion: An Electro-Photographic Investigation of Consecutive Phases of Animal Movements by Eadweard Muybridge Published under the Auspices of the University of Pennsylvania. Prospectus and Catalogue of Plates (Philadelphia, 1887)

Animals in Motion: An Electro-Photographic Investigation of Consecutive Phases of Animal Progressive Movements (London, 1899, 1901, 1902, 1907, 1918, 1925)

The Attitudes of Animals in Motion. A Series of Photographs Illustrating the Consecutive Positions Assumed by Animals Performing Various Movements: Executed at Palo Alto, California, in 1878 and 1879 (1881). Album of original photographs

'The Attitudes of Animals in Motion', *Journal of the Franklin Institute*, 115, no. 4 (April 1883), pp. 260–74. Transcript of lecture, Franklin Institute, 13 February 1883

Catalogue of Photographic Views Illustrating the Yosemite, Mammoth Trees, Geyser Springs, and Other Remarkable and Interesting Scenery of the Far West by Muybridge (San Francisco, 1873)

Descriptive Zoopraxography; or, The Science of Animal Locomotion Made Popular, by Eadweard Muybridge. Published as a Memento of a Series of Lectures Given by the Author under the Auspices of the United States Government, Bureau of Education, at the World's Columbian Exposition, in Zoopraxographical Hall, 1893 (Philadelphia, 1893)

The Human Figure in Motion: An Electro-Photographic Investigation of Consecutive Phases of Muscular Actions (London, 1901, 1904, 1907, 1913, 1919, 1931)

'Leland Stanford's Gift to Art and to Science: Mr Muybridge's Inventions of
    Instant Photography and the Marvelous Zoogyroscope', *San Francisco
    Examiner*, 6 February 1881, p. 3
'A New Sky Shade', *Philadelphia Photographer*, 6, no. 65 (May 1869) pp. 142–4
'"Occident" Photographed at Full Speed', *Daily Alta California*, 3 August 1877
'Photographing Animals in Action', *Philadelphia Photographer*, 16, no. 181
    (January 1879), p. 71
'Pneumatic Clocks', Letter, *Scientific American*, 40, no. 13 (29 March 1879),
    p. 196
*Prospectus of a New and Elaborate Work upon the Attitudes of Man, the Horse
    and Other Animals in Motion* (New York, 1883)
*The Science of Animal Locomotion (Zoopraxography): An Electro-Photographic
    Investigation of Consecutive Phases of Animal Movements by Eadweard
    Muybridge Executed and Published under the Auspices of the University of
    Pennsylvania* (Philadelphia, 1891–92)

Works on Muybridge

Brookman, Philip, ed. *Helios: Eadweard Muybridge in a Time of Change*, exh.
    cat., Corcoran Gallery of Art, Washington, DC (Washington, DC and
    Göttingen, 2010)
Burns, E. Bradford, *Eadweard Muybridge in Guatemala, 1875: The Photographer
    as Social Recorder* (Berkeley, CA, 1986)
Clegg, Brian, *The Man Who Stopped Time: The Illuminating Story of Eadweard
    Muybridge – Pioneer Photographer, Father of the Motion Picture, Murderer*
    (Washington, DC, 2007)
Coe, Brian, *Muybridge and the Chronophotographers* (London, 1992)
Haas, Robert Bartlett, *Muybridge: Man in Motion* (Berkeley, CA, 1976)
Harris, David, with Eric Sandweiss, *Eadweard Muybridge and the Photographic
    Panorama of San Francisco, 1850–1880*, exh. cat., Canadian Center for
    Architecture, Montreal (Cambridge, MA, 1993)
Hendricks, Gordon, *Eadweard Muybridge: The Father of the Motion Picture*
    (New York, 1975)
Herbert, Stephen, ed., *Eadweard Muybridge: The Kingston Museum Bequest*
    (Hastings, 2004)
Hill, Paul, *Eadweard Muybridge* (London, 2001)

Klett, Mark, *One City / Two Visions: San Francisco Panoramas, 1878 and 1990* (San Francisco, 1990)

MacDonnell, Kevin, *Eadweard Muybridge: The Man Who Invented the Moving Picture* (Boston, MA, 1972)

Marks, William Dennis, Harrison Allen, and Francis X. Dercum. *Animal Locomotion: The Muybridge Work at the University of Pennsylvania—The Method and the Result* (Philadelphia, 1888)

Martini, John A, *Eadweard Muybridge & James D. Givens: Photographers of the Golden Gate* (Fairfax, CA, 2000)

McBain, Robert S., *San Francisco 1878: Portrait of the City by Eadweard Muybridge* (San Francisco, 1979)

Mozley, Anita Ventura, Robert Bartlett Haas, and Françoise Forster-Hahn, *Eadweard Muybridge: The Stanford Years, 1872–1882* (Stanford, CA, 1972)

Muñoz, Luis Luján, *Fotografías de Eduardo Santiago Muybridge en Guatamala, 1875* (Guatamala City, 1984)

—, *Guatamala – 1875: Fotografías de Eduardo Santiago Muybridge* (Guatamala City, 1975)

Prodger, Philip, ed. *Time Stands Still: Muybridge and the Instantaneous Photography Movement* (New York, 2003)

Sheldon, James L., and Jock Reynolds, *Motion and Document, Sequence and Time*: *Eadweard Muybridge and Contemporary American Photography* (Andover, MA, 1991)

Solnit, Rebecca, *River of Shadows: Eadweard Muybridge and the Technological Wild West* (New York, 2003)

Stillman, Jacob Davis Babcock, *The Horse in Motion as Shown by Instantaneous Photography with a Study on Animal Mechanics Founded on Anatomy and the Revelations of the Camera, in which is Demonstrated the Theory of Quadrupedal Locomotion*, Executed under the auspices of Leland Standford (Boston, 1882)

Articles on Muybridge

Braun, Marta, 'Muybridge's Scientific Fictions', in *Studies in Visual Communication*, 10, no. 3 (Summer 1984), pp. 2–22

—, 'Muybridge's *Animal Locomotion*: The Director's Cut', *History of Photography*, 24, no. 1 (Spring 2000), pp. 52–4

—, and Elizabeth Whitcombe, 'Marey, Muybridge, and Londe: The
    Photography of Pathological Locomotion', *History of Photography*,
    23, no. 3 (Autumn 1999), pp. 218–24

Brown, Elspeth H., 'Racialising the Virile Body: Eadweard Muybridge's
    Locomotion Studies, 1883–1887', *Gender & History*, 17, no. 3 (November
    2005), pp. 627–56

Frampton, Hollis, 'Eadweard Muybridge: Fragments of a Tesseract', in *Circles
    of Confusion: Film, Photography, Video, Texts, 1968–1980* (Rochester, NY,
    1983)

Gordon, Sarah, 'Prestige, Professionalism, and the Paradox of Eadweard
    Muybridge's *Animal Locomotion* Nudes', *Pennsylvania Magazine of
    History and Biography*, 130, no. 1 (January 2006), pp. 79–104

—, 'Out of Sequence: Suspended and Spectacular Bodies in Eadweard
    Muybridge's Animal Locomotion Series', *Spectator*, xxviii/2 (Spring
    2008), pp. 10–22

Hamilton, Harlan, '"Les Allures du Cheval": Eadweard James Muybridge's
    Contribution to the Motion Picture', *Film Comment*, 5, no. 3 (Fall 1969),
    pp. 16–35

Homer, William I., with John Talbot, 'Eakins, Muybridge, and the Motion
    Picture Process', *Art Quarterly*, 26, no. 2 (Summer 1963), pp. 194–216

Hood, Mary V. Jessup, and Robert Bartlett Haas, 'Eadweard Muybridge's
    Yosemite Valley Photographs, 1867–1872', *California Historical Society
    Quarterly*, 43 (March 1963), pp. 5–26

'The Last of the Modocs', *Harper's Weekly* (21 June 1873), pp. 532–4

Mileaf, Janine A., 'Poses for the Camera: Eadweard Muybridge's Studies
    of the Human Figure', *American Art*, 16, no. 3 (Fall 2002), pp. 31–53

Morgan, Jayne, 'Eadweard Muybridge and W. S. Playfair: An Aesthetics
    of Neurasthenia', *History of Photography*, 23, no. 3 (Autumn 1999),
    pp. 225–31

Mozley, Anita Ventura, 'Introduction', in *Muybridge's Complete Human and
    Animal Locomotion* (New York, 1979), vol. I, pp. vii–xxxviii

Ott, John, 'Iron Horses: Leland Stanford, Eadweard Muybridge and the
    Industrialised Eye', *Oxford Art Journal*, xxviii/3 (2005), pp. 407–28

Palmquist, Peter, 'Imagemakers of the Modoc War: Louis Heller and
    Eadweard Muybridge', *Journal of California Anthropology*, 4, no. 2
    (Winter 1977), pp. 206–41

Shimamura, Arthur P., 'Muybridge in Motion: Travels in Art, Psychology, and Neurology', *History of Photography*, 26, no. 4 (Winter 2002), pp. 341–50

Books and Articles relevant to Muybridge

Braun, Marta, *Picturing Time: The Work of Étienne-Jules Marey (1830–1904)* (Chicago, 1992)

Danly, Susan, and Cheryl Leibold, eds, *Eakins and the Photograph: Works by Thomas Eakins and his Circle in the Collection of the Pennsylvania Academy of the Fine Arts* (Washington, DC, 1994)

Edwards, Elizabeth, ed, *Anthropology and Photography, 1860–1920* (New Haven, CT, 1992)

Gotlieb, Marc, *The Plight of Emulation: Ernest Meissonier and French Salon Painting* (Princeton, NJ, 1996)

Kelsey, Robin, *Archive Style, Photographs, and Illustrations for U.S. Surveys, 1850–1890* (Berkeley, CA, 2007)

Kibbey, Mead B., *The Railroad Photographs of Alfred A. Hart, Artist* (Sacramento, CA, 1996)

Marey, Étienne-Jules, *Animal Mechanism: A Treatise on Terrestial and Aerial Locomotion* (New York, 1874)

Palmquist, Peter E., and Thomas R. Kailbourn, *Pioneer Photographers of the Far West: A Biographical Dictionary, 1840–1865* (Stanford, CA, 2000)

Rejlander, Oscar Gustave, 'On Photographing Horses', *British Journal Photographic Almanac* (1872–3), p. 115

Rossell, Deac, *Ottomar Anschütz and his Electrical Wonder* (Hastings, 1997)

Sandweiss, Martha, *Print the Legend: Photography and the American West* (New Haven, CT, and London, 2002)

Schwartz, Vanessa R., *Spectacular Realities: Early Mass Culture in Fin-de-Siècle Paris* (Berkeley, CA, 1998)

Williams, Linda, *Hard Core: Power, Pleasure, and the 'Frenzy of the Visible'* (Berkeley, CA, 1999)

Acknowledgements

I am grateful to Vivian Constantinopoulos for commissioning this book and to her colleagues at Reaktion Books, Robert Williams and Harry Gilonis, for so cheerfully working with me on it. I owe much to friends and colleagues for their support, and for their interest and assistance in different aspects of this work: Elspeth Brown, Kaitlin Booher, Phillip Brookman, Peta Cook, Michelle Delaney, Thierry Gervais, David Harris, Paul Herzmann, Corey Keller, Mead Kibbey, Hope Kingsley, Gail and Barry Lord, Susan Oxtoby, Shannon Perich, Mary Panzer, Michelle Piranio, Emma Rummins, Deac Rossell, Jan Roberts, Rebecca Solnit, Mary-jo Stevenson, Eleanor Wachtel, Leonard Walle and David Whillans.

Without the patience, knowledge and kindness of Martha Fay, my sister Anita Agar, and my colleagues-in-Muybridge Stephen Herbert and Joel Snyder, this book could not have been written. My husband, Edward Epstein saw it through. Susan Patrick, Lucina Fraser and the library staff at Ryerson made it possible.

Photo Acknowledgements

The author and publishers wish to express their thanks to the below sources of illustrative material and/or permission to reproduce it:

Archives of American Art, Smithsonian Institution, Washington, DC: p. 187; collection of the author p. 162; The Bancroft Library, University of California, Berkeley: pp. 47, 63, 104, 108; Museum of Fine Arts, Boston: p. 6; California Historical Society, San Francisco: p. 96; The J. Paul Getty Museum, Malibu, CA: p. 76; courtesy of Susan Herzig & Paul Hertzmann (Paul M. Hertzmann, Inc., San Francisco): pp. 37, 55, 61, 66, 74, 79, 81, 86; reproduced by permission of Kingston Museum and Heritage Service: p. 154; Library of Congress, Washington, DC (Prints & Photographs Division): pp. 129, 139, 144–45, 156–7; Metropolitan Museum of Art, New York (Department of Prints and Photographs – Harris Brisbane Dick Fund, 1946): p. 140; digital image © 2010 The Museum of Modern Art, New York/Licensed by SCALA/Art Resource, New York: pp. 102–3; from Eadweard Muybridge, *Animal Locomotion: An Electro-Photographic Investigation of Consecutive Phases of Animal Movements 1872–1885* (Philadelphia, 1887): pp. 190–91, 192, 194–95, 200–1, 208–9, 210–11, 213–14; from Muybridge's album of original photographs entitled *The Attitudes of Animals in Motion: A Series of Photographs Illustrating the Consecutive Positions Assumed by Animals in Performing Various Movements; Executed at Palo Alto, California, in 1878 and 1879*: pp. 139, 140, 156–7; from Muybridge, T*he Human Figure in Motion . . . An Electro-Photographic Investigation of Consecutive Phases of Muscular Actions* (London, 1901): pp. 232, 233; from Muybridge, *The Pacific Coast of Central America and Mexico; the Isthmus of Panama; Guatemala; and the Cultivation and Shipment of Coffee* (San Francisco, 1876): pp. 102–3; National Museum of American Art, Smithsonian Institution, Washington, DC: pp. 204–5; San Francisco Public

Library (San Francisco History Center): p. 117; Science Museum, London: p. 160; Stanford University Archives, Stanford, CA (Stanford Historical Photograph Collection): p. 69; photo Toronto Reference Library: p. 225; University of Michigan (William L. Clemens Library): p. 164; from the collection of Leonard A. Walle: pp. 33, 35, 51, 57, 62, 73, 83, 109, 110; Wilson Centre for Photography, London: pp. 126, 127.